James David Hart, Donald Grant Mitchell

Reveries of a Bachelor

A Book of the Heart

James David Hart, Donald Grant Mitchell

Reveries of a Bachelor

A Book of the Heart

ISBN/EAN: 9783744666268

Printed in Europe, USA, Canada, Australia, Japan

Cover: Foto ©Andreas Hilbeck / pixelio.de

More available books at **www.hansebooks.com**

REVERIES

OF

A BACHELOR.

OR

A BOOK OF THE HEART.

By IK MARVEL.

It is worth the labor — saith Plotinus — *to consider well of Love, whether it be a God. or a divell, or passion of the minde, or partly God, partly divell, partly passion.* — BURTON'S ANATOMY OF MELANCHOLY, Part III. Sec. 1.

A NEW EDITION.

NEW YORK:
CHARLES SCRIBNER'S SONS.
1880.

Entered according to Act of Congress, in the year 1863, by
CHARLES SCRIBNER & Co.,
In the Clerk's Office of the District Court of the United States for the Southern District of New York

RIVERSIDE, CAMBRIDGE:
STEREOTYPED AND PRINTED BY
H. O. HOUGHTON AND COMPANY

TO

ONE AT HOME,

IN WHOM ARE MET SO MANY OF THE GRACES AND

THE VIRTUES, OF WHICH AS BACHELOR

I DREAMED,

THIS NEW EDITION OF MY BOOK

IS DEDICATED.

A NEW PREFACE.

MY publisher has written me that the old type of this book of the Reveries are so far worn and battered, that they will bear no further usage; and, in view of a new edition, he asks for such revision of the text as I may deem judicious, and for a few lines in way of preface.

I began the revision. I scored out word after word; presently I came to the scoring out of paragraphs; and before I had done, I was making my scores by the page.

It would never do. It might be the better, but it would not be the same. I cannot lop away those twelve swift, changeful years that are gone.

Middle age does not look on life like youth; we cannot make it. And why mix the years and the thoughts? Let the young carry their own burdens, and banner; and we — ours.

I have determined not to touch the book. A race has grown up which may welcome its youngness, and find a spirit or a sentiment in it that cleaves to them, and cheers them, and is true. I hope they will.

For me those young years are gone. I cannot go

back to that tide. I hear the rush of it in quiet hours, like the murmur of lost music. The companions who discussed with me these little fantasies as they came reeking from the press, — and suggested how I might have mended matters by throwing in a new light here, or deepening the shadows there, — are no longer within ear-shot. If living, they are widely scattered; — heads of young families, maybe, who will bring now to the re-reading of passages they thought too sombre, the light of such bitter experience as, ten years since, neither they nor I had fathomed. Others are dapper, elderly bachelors, — coquetting with the world in the world's great cities, — brisk in their step, — coaxing all the features of youth to stay by them, — brushing their hair with needless and nervous frequency over the growing spot of baldness, — perversely reckoning themselves still proper mates for girlhood, — dreaming yet (as we once dreamed together) of an Elysium in store, and of a fairy future, where only roses shall bloom.

The houses where I was accustomed to linger show other faces at the windows, — bright and cheery faces, it is true, — but they are looking over at a young fellow upon the other side of the way.

The children who sat for my pictures are grown; the boys I watched at their game of taw, and who clapped their hands gleefully at a good shot, are buttoned into natty blue frocks, and wear little lace-bordered bands upon their shoulders; and over and over, as I read my morning paper, I am brought to sudden pause, and a strange electric current thrills me, as I come upon their boy-names printed in the dead-roll of the war.

The girls who wore the charming white pinafores, and a wild tangle of flaxen curls, have now netted up all those clustering tresses into a stately Pompadour head-dress; and they rustle past me in silks, and do not know me.

The elderly friends who cheered me with kindly expressions of look and tongue — I am compelled to say — now trip in their speech; and I observe a little morocco case at their elbows — for eye-glasses.

And as they put them on, to read what I may be saying now, let them keep their old charity, and think as well of me as they can.

EDGEWOOD, 1863.

PREFACE.

THIS book is neither more nor less than it pretends to be: it is a collection of those floating Reveries which have, from time to time, drifted across my brain. I never yet met with a bachelor who had not his share of just such floating visions; and the only difference between us lies in the fact that I have tossed them from me in the shape of a Book.

If they had been worked over with more unity of design, I dare say I might have made a respectable novel; as it is, I have chosen the honester way of setting them down as they came seething from my thought, with all their crudities and contrasts, uncovered.

As for the truth that is in them, the world may believe what it likes; for having written to humor the world, it would be hard if I should curtail any of its privileges of judgment. I should think there was as much truth in them as in most Reveries.

The first story of the book has already had some publicity; and the criticisms upon it have amused and pleased me. One honest journalist avows that it could never have been written by a bachelor. I thank him for thinking so well of me, and heartily wish that his thought were as true as it is kind.

Yet I am inclined to think that bachelors are the only safe and secure observers of all the phases of married life. The rest of the world have their hobbies, and by law, as well as by immemorial custom, are reckoned unfair witnesses in everything relating to their matrimonial affairs.

Perhaps I ought however to make an exception in favor of spinsters, who, like us, are independent spectators, and possess just that kind of indifference to the marital state which makes them intrepid in their observations, and very desirable for — authorities.

As for the style of the book, I have nothing to say for it, except to refer to my title. These are not sermons, nor essays, nor criticisms; — they are only Reveries. And if the reader should stumble upon occasional magniloquence, or be worried with a little too much of sentiment, pray let him remember — that I am dreaming

But while I say this in the hope of nicking off the wiry edge of my reader's judgment, I shall yet stand up boldly for the general tone and character of the book. If there is bad feeling in it, or insincerity, or shallow sentiment, or any foolish depth of affection betrayed, — I am responsible; and the critics may expose it to their heart's content.

I have moreover a kindly feeling for these Reveries, from their very private character: they consist mainly of just such whimseys, and reflections, as a great many brother bachelors are apt to indulge in, but which they are too cautious, or too prudent, to lay before the world. As I have in this matter shown a frankness and *naïveté* which are unusual, I shall ask a corresponding frankness in my reader; and I can assure him safely that this is eminently one of those books which were "never intended for publication."

In the hope that this plain avowal may quicken the reader's charity, and screen me from cruel judgment.

I remain, with sincere good wishes,

IK MARVEL.

NEW YORK, *Nov.* 1850.

CONTENTS.

FIRST REVERIE.

	PAGE
OVER A WOOD-FIRE	17
I. SMOKE — SIGNIFYING DOUBT	21
II. BLAZE — SIGNIFYING CHEER	30
III. ASHES — SIGNIFYING DESOLATION	37

SECOND REVERIE.

BY A CITY GRATE	53
I. SEA-COAL	60
II. ANTHRACITE	77

THIRD REVERIE.

OVER HIS CIGAR	95
I. LIGHTED WITH A COAL	99
II. LIGHTED WITH A WISP OF PAPER	112
III. LIGHTED WITH A MATCH	126

FOURTH REVERIE.

MORNING, NOON, AND EVENING	141
I. MORNING — WHICH IS THE PAST	148
SCHOOL-DAYS	157
THE SEA	168
THE FATHER-LAND	175
A ROMAN GIRL	184
THE APENNINES	194
ENRICA	202

CONTENTS.

	PAGE
II. NOON — WHICH IS THE PRESENT	210
EARLY FRIENDS	212
SCHOOL REVISITED	220
COLLEGE	225
THE PACKET OF BELLA.	232
III. EVENING — WHICH IS THE FUTURE	241
CARRY	245
THE LETTER	253
NEW TRAVEL.	259
HOME.	271

FIRST REVERIE.

SMOKE, FLAME, AND ASHES.

OVER A WOOD-FIRE.

I HAVE got a quiet farm-house in the country, a very humble place to be sure, tenanted by a worthy enough man, of the old New-England stamp, where I sometimes go for a day or two in the winter, to look over the farm accounts, and to see how the stock is thriving on the winter's keep.

One side the door, as you enter from the porch, is a little parlor, scarce twelve feet by ten, with a cosy-looking fireplace, a heavy oak floor, a couple of arm-chairs, and a brown table with carved lions' feet. Out of this room opens a little cabinet, only big enough for a broad bachelor bedstead, where I sleep upon feathers, and wake in the morning with my eye upon a saucy colored lithographic print of some fancy " Bessy."

It happens to be the only house in the world of which I am *bona-fide* owner; and I take a vast deal of comfort in treating it just as I choose. I manage to break some article of furniture, almost every time I pay it a visit; and if I cannot open the window readily of a morning, to breathe the fresh air, I knock out a pane or two of glass with my boot. I lean against the walls in a very old arm-chair there is on the premises, and scarce ever fail to worry such a hole in the plastering as would set me down for a round charge for damages in town, or make a prim housewife fret herself into a raging fever. I laugh out loud with myself, in my big arm-chair, when I think that I am neither afraid of one nor the other.

As for the fire, I keep the little hearth so hot as to warm half the cellar below, and the whole space between the jambs roars for hours together with white flame. To be sure, the windows are not very tight, between broken panes and bad joints, so that the fire, large as it is, is by no means an extravagant comfort.

As night approaches, I have a huge pile of oak and hickory placed beside the hearth; I put out the tallow candle on the mantel, (using the family snuffers, with one leg broke,) then, drawing my chair directly in front of the blazing wood, and setting one foot on each of the old iron fire-dogs, (until they grow too warm,) I dispose myself for an evening of such sober and thoughtful quietude, as I believe, on my soul, that very few of my fellow-men have the good fortune to enjoy.

My tenant, meantime, in the other room, I can hear now and then, though there is a thick stone chimney and broad entry between, multiplying contrivances with his wife to put two babies to sleep. This occupies them, I should say, usually an hour; though my only measure of time (for I never carry a watch into the country) is the blaze of my fire. By ten, or thereabouts, my stock of wood is nearly exhausted; I pile upon the hot coals what remains, and sit watching how it kindles, and blazes, and goes out, — even like our joys! — and then slip by the light of the embers into my bed, where I luxuriate in such sound and healthful slumber as only such rattling window-frames, and country air, can supply.

But to return. The other evening, — it happened to be on my last visit to my farm-house, — when I had exhausted all the ordinary rural topics of thought, had formed all sorts of conjectures as to the income of the year; had planned a new wall around one lot, and the clearing up of another, now covered with patriarchal wood; and wondered if the little rickety house would not be after all a snug enough box to live and to die in, — I fell on a sudden into such an unprecedented line of thought, which took such deep hold of my sympathies — sometimes even starting tears — that I determined, the next day, to set as much of it as I could recall, on paper.

Something — it may have been the home-looking blaze, (I am a bachelor of — say six and twenty,) or possibly a plaintive cry of the baby in my tenant's room — had suggested to me the thought of — Marriage.

I piled upon the heated fire-dogs the last armful of my wood; and now, said I, bracing myself courageously between the arms of my chair, I'll not flinch; I'll pursue the thought wherever it leads, though it lead me to the d———, (I am apt to be hasty,) — at least, continued I, softening, until my fire is out.

The wood was green, and at first showed no disposition to blaze. It smoked furiously. Smoke, thought I, always goes before blaze; and so does doubt go before decision: and my Reverie, from that very starting point, slipped into this shape: —

I.

Smoke — Signifying Doubt.

A WIFE? — thought I; — yes, a wife!
And why!

And pray, my dear sir, why not — why? Why not doubt; why not hesitate; why not tremble?

Does a man buy a ticket in a lottery — a poor man, whose whole earnings go in to secure the ticket — without trembling, hesitating, and doubting?

Can a man stake his bachelor respectability, his independence and comfort, upon the die of absorbing, unchanging, relentless marriage, without trembling at the venture?

Shall a man who has been free to chase his fancies over the wide world, without let or hindrance, shut himself up to marriage-ship, within four walls called Home, that are to claim him, his time, his trouble, and his tears, thenceforward forevermore, without doubts thick, and thick-coming as Smoke?

Shall he who has been hitherto a mere observer of other men's cares and business, — moving off where they made him sick of heart, approaching whenever and wherever they made him gleeful, — shall he now undertake administration of just such cares and business, without qualms? Shall he, whose whole life has been but a nimble succession of escapes from trifling difficulties, now broach without doubtings — that Matrimony, where if difficulty beset him, there is no escape. Shall this brain of mine, careless-working, never tired with idleness, feeding on long vagaries and high gigantic castles, dreaming out beatitudes hour by hour, — turn itself at length to such dull task-work, as thinking out a livelihood for wife and children?

Where thenceforward will be those sunny dreams in which I have warmed my fancies and my heart, and lighted my eye with crystal? This very marriage, which a brilliant working imagination has invested time and again with brightness and delight, can serve no longer as a mine for teeming fancy: all, alas! will be gone — reduced to the dull standard of the actual! No more room for intrepid forays of imagination — no more gorgeous realm-making — all will be over!

Why not, I thought, go on dreaming?

Can any wife be prettier than an after-dinner fancy, idle and yet vivid, can paint for you? Can any children make less noise than the little, rosy-cheeked ones, who have no existence except in the *omnium gatherum* of your own brain? Can any housewife be more unex ceptionable than she who goes sweeping daintily the cobwebs that gather in your dreams? Can any domestic larder be better stocked than the private larder of your head dozing on a cushioned chair-back at Delmonico's? Can any family purse be better filled than the exceeding plump one you dream of, after reading such pleasant books as Münchhausen, or Typee?

But if, after all, it must be, — duty, or what-not, making provocation, — what then? And I clapped my feet hard against the fire-dogs, and leaned back, and turned my face to the ceiling, as much as to say, — And where on earth, then, shall a poor devil look for a wife?

Somebody says, Lyttleton or Shaftesbury I think, that "marriages would be happier if they were all arranged by the Lord Chancellor." Unfortunately, we have no Lord Chancellor to make this commutation of our misery.

Shall a man then scour the country on a mule's back, like Honest Gil Blas of Santillane; or shall he make application to some such intervening providence as Madame St. Marc, who, as I see by the *Presse*, manages these matters to one's hand for some five per cent. on the fortunes of the parties?

I have trouted, when the brook was so low, and the sky so hot, that I might as well have thrown my fly upon the turnpike; and I have hunted hare at noon, and woodcock in snow-time, never despairing, scarce doubting; but for a poor hunter of his kind, without traps or snares, or any aid of police or constabulary, to traverse the world, where are swarming, on a moderate computation, some three hundred and odd millions of unmarried women, for a single capture — irremediable, unchangeable — and yet a capture which, by strange metonymy not laid down in the books, is very apt to turn captor into captive, and make game of hunter, — all this, surely, surely may make a man shrug with doubt!

Then, again, — there are the plaguey wife's relations. Who knows how many third, fourth, or fifth cousins will appear at careless complimentary intervals, long after you had settled into the placid belief that all congratulatory visits were at an end? How many twisted-headed brothers will be putting in their advice, as a friend to Peggy?

How many maiden aunts will come to spend a month or two with their "dear Peggy," and want to know every tea-time "if she is n't a dear love of a wife?" Then, dear father-in-law will beg (taking dear Peggy's hand in his) to give a little wholesome counsel; and will be very sure to advise just the contrary of what you had determined to undertake. And dear mamma-in-law must set her nose into Peggy's cupboard, and insist upon having the key to your own private locker in the wainscot.

Then, perhaps, there is a little bevy of dirty-nosed nephews who come to spend the holidays, and eat up your East India sweetmeats; and who are forever tramping over your head, or raising the old Harry below, while you are busy with your clients. Last, and worst, is some fidgety old uncle, forever too cold or too hot, who vexes you with his patronizing airs, and impudently kisses his little Peggy!

—— That could be borne, however; for perhaps he has promised his fortune to Peggy. Peggy, then, will be rich: (and the thought made me rub my shins, which were now getting comfortably warm upon the fire-dogs.) Then, she will be forever talking of *her* fortune; and pleasantly reminding you, on occasion of a favorite purchase, how lucky that *she* had the means; and dropping hints about economy; and buying very extravagant Paisleys.

She will annoy you by looking over the stock-list at breakfast-time; and mention quite carelessly to your clients that she is interested in *such* or such a speculation.

She will be provokingly silent when you hint to a tradesman that you have not the money by you for his small bill; in short, she will tear the life out of you, making you pay in righteous retribution of annoyance, grief, vexation, shame, and sickness of heart, for the superlative folly of "marrying rich."

—— But if not rich, then poor. Bah! the thought made me stir the coals; but there was still no blaze. The paltry earnings you are able to wring out of clients by the sweat of your brow, will now be all *our* income; you will be pestered for pin-money, and pestered with your poor wife's relations. Ten to one, she will stickle about taste, — " Sir Visto's," — and want to make this so pretty, and that so charming, if she *only* had the means; and is sure Paul (a kiss) can't deny his little Peggy such a trifling sum, and all for the common benefit.

Then she, for one, means that *her* children sha'n't go a-begging for clothes, — and another pull at the purse. Trust a poor mother to dress her children in finery!

Perhaps she is ugly; not noticeable at first, but growing on her, and (what is worse) growing faster on you. You wonder why you did n't see that vulgar nose long ago; and that lip — it is very strange, you think, that you ever thought it pretty. And then, to come to breakfast, with her hair looking as it does, and you not so much as daring to say, " Peggy, *do* brush your hair!" Her foot too — not very bad when decently *chaussée* — but now since she's married she does wear such infernal slippers! And yet for all this, to be prigging up for an hour when any of my old chums come to dine with me!

'Bless your kind hearts my dear fellows," said I thrusting the tongs into the coals, and speaking out loud, as if my voice could reach from Virginia to Paris: " not married yet!"

Perhaps Peggy is pretty enough, only shrewish.

—— No matter for cold coffee; you should have been up before.

What sad, thin, poorly cooked chops, to eat with your rolls!

—— She thinks they are very good, and wonders how you can set such an example to your children.

The butter is nauseating.

—— She has no other, and hopes you'll not raise a storm about butter a little turned. I think I see myself, ruminated I, sitting meekly at table, scarce daring to lift up my eyes, utterly fagged out with some quarrel of yesterday, choking down detestably sour muffins, that my wife thinks are "delicious," slipping in dried mouthfuls of burnt ham off the side of my fork tines, slipping off my chair sideways at the end, and slipping out, with my hat between my knees, to business, and never feeling myself a competent, sound-minded man, till the oak door is between me and Peggy.

—— "Ha, ha! not yet," said I; and in so earnest a tone that my dog started to his feet, cocked his eye to have a good look into my face, met my smile of triumph with an amiable wag of the tail, and curled up again in the corne-

Again, Peggy is rich enough, well enough, mild enough, only she does n't care a fig for you. She has married you because father or grandfather thought the match eligible, and because she did n't wish to disoblige them. Besides, she did n't positively hate you, and thought you were a respectable enough young person; she has told you so repeatedly at dinner. She wonders you like to read poetry; she wishes you would buy her a good cook-book, and insists upon your making your will at the birth of the first baby.

She thinks Captain So-and-So a splendid-looking fellow, and wishes you would trim up a little, were it only for appearance' sake.

You need not hurry up from the office so early at night: she, bless her dear heart! does not feel lonely You read to her a love-tale: she interrupts the pathetic parts with directions to her seamstress. You read of marriages: she sighs, and asks if Captain So-and-So has left town! She hates to be mewed up in a cottage, or between brick walls; she does *so* love the Springs !

But, again, Peggy loves you; at least she swears it, with her hand on the " Sorrows of Werther." She has pin-money which she spends for the " Literary World " and the " Friends in Council." She is not bad-looking save a bit too much of forehead; nor is she sluttish, unless a *negligé* till three o'clock, and an ink-stain on the forefinger be sluttish; but then she is such a sad blue !

SMOKE — SIGNIFYING DOUBT.   29

You never fancied, when you saw her buried in a three-volume novel, that it was anything more than a girlish vagary; and when she quoted Latin, you thought innocently that she had a capital memory for her samplers.

But to be bored eternally about divine Danté and funny Goldoni, is too bad. Your copy of Tasso, a treasure print of 1680, is all bethumbed and dogs-eared, and spotted with baby-gruel. Even your Seneca — an Elzevir — is all sweaty with handling. She adores La Fontaine, reads Balzac with a kind of artist-scowl, and will not let Greek alone.

You hint at broken rest and an aching head at breakfast, and she will fling you a scrap of Anthology, in lieu of the camphor-bottle, or chant the αἰαῖ, αἰαῖ, of tragic chorus.

—— The nurse is getting dinner; you are holding the baby; Peggy is reading Bruyère.

The fire smoked thick as pitch, and puffed out little clouds over the chimney-piece. I gave the fore-stick a kick, at the thought of Peggy, baby, and Bruyère.

—— Suddenly the flame flickered bluely athwart the smoke, caught at a twig below, rolled round the mossy oak stick, twined among the crackling tree-limbs, mounted, lit up the whole body of smoke, and blazed out cheerily and bright. Doubt vanished with **Smoke**, and Hope began with Flame.

II.

Blaze — Signifying Cheer.

I PUSHED my chair back; drew up another; stretched out my feet cosily upon it, rested my elbows on the chair-arms, leaned my head on one hand, and looked straight into the leaping and dancing flame.

—— Love is a flame, ruminated I; and (glancing round the room) how a flame brightens up a man's habitation.

"Carlo," said I, calling up my dog into the light; "good fellow, Carlo!" and I patted him kindly; and he wagged his tail, and laid his nose across my knee, and looked wistfully up in my face; then strode away, turned to look again, and lay down to sleep.

"Pho, the brute!" said I; "it is not enough, after all, to like a dog."

—— If now in that chair yonder, not the one your feet lie upon, but the other, beside you, — closer yet, — were seated a sweet-faced girl, with a pretty little foot lying out upon the hearth, a bit of lace running round the swelling throat, the hair parted to a charm over a forehead fair as any of your dreams, — and if you could reach an arm round that chair-back, without fear of giving offence, and suffer your fingers to play idly with those curls that escape down the neck, — and if you could clasp with your other hand those little, white, taper fingers of hers, which lie so temptingly within reach, and so, talk softly and low in presence of the blaze, while the hours slip without knowledge, and the winter winds whistle uncared for, — if, in short, you were no bachelor, but the husband of some such sweet image, (dream, call it rather,) would it not be far pleasanter than this cold, single, night-sitting, counting the sticks. reckoning the length of the blaze, and the height of the falling snow?

And if, some or all of those wild vagaries that grow on your fancy at such an hour, you could whisper into listening because loving ears, — ears not tired with listening, because it is you who whisper, — ears ever indulgent, because eager to praise, — and if your darkest fancies were lit up, not merely with bright wood-fire, but with a ringing laugh of that sweet face turned up in fond rebuke, — how far better, than to be waxing black and sour over pestilential humors, alone, — your very dog asleep?

And if, when a glowing thought comes into your brain, quick and sudden, you could tell it over as to a second self, to that sweet creature, who is not away, because she loves to be there; and if you could watch the thought catching that girlish mind, illuming that fair brow, sparkling in those pleasantest of eyes, — how far better than to feel it slumbering, and going out, heavy, lifeless, and dead, in your own selfish fancy. And if a generous emotion steals over you, coming you know not whither, would there not be a richer charm in lavishing it in caress, or endearing word, upon that fondest and most dear one, than in patting your glossy coated dog, or sinking lonely to smiling slumbers?

How would not benevolence ripen with such monitor to task it! How would not selfishness grow faint and dull, leaning ever to that second self, which is the loved one! How would not guile shiver, and grow weak, before that girl-brow, and eye of innocence! How would not all that boyhood prized of enthusiasm, and quick blood, and life, renew itself in such presence!

The fire was getting hotter, and I moved into the middle of the room. The shadows the flames made were playing like fairy forms over floor, and wall, and ceiling.

My fancy would surely quicken, thought I, if such being were in attendance. Surely imagination would be stronger and purer, if it could have the playful fancies of dawning womanhood to delight it. All toil would be torn from mind-labor, if but another heart grew into this present soul, quickening it, warming it cheering it, bidding it ever God speed!

Her face would make a halo, rich as a rainbow, atop of all such noisome things as we lonely souls call trouble. Her smile would illumine the blackest of crowding cares: and darkness that now seats you despondent in your solitary chair for days together, weaving bitter fancies, dreaming bitter dreams, would grow light and thin, and spread and float away, chased by that beloved smile.

Your friend — poor fellow! — dies: never mind, that gentle clasp of *her* fingers, as she steals behind you, telling you not to weep, — it is worth ten friends!

Your sister, sweet one, is dead—buried. The worms are busy with all her fairness. How it makes you think earth nothing but a spot to dig graves upon!

—— It is more. *She*, she says, will be a sister; and the waving curls, as she leans upon your shoulder, touch your cheek, and your wet eye turns to meet those other eyes — God has sent his angel, surely!

Your mother, alas for it, she is gone! Is there any bitterness to a youth, alone and homeless, like this!

But you are not homeless; you are not alone: *she* is there; her tears softening yours, her smile lighting yours, her grief killing yours; and you live again, to assuage that kind sorrow of hers.

Then, those children, rosy, fair-haired; no, they do not disturb you with their prattle now; they are yours! Toss away there on the greensward; never mind the hyacinths, the snowdrops, the violets, if so be any are there; the perfume of their healthful lips is worth all the flowers of the world. No need now to gather wild bouquets to love and cherish: flower, tree, gun, are all dead things; things livelier hold your soul.

And she, the mother, sweetest and fairest of all, watching, tending, caressing, loving, till your own heart grows pained with tenderest jealousy, and cures itself with loving.

You have no need now of any cold lecture to teach thankfulness: your heart is full of it. No need now, as once, of bursting blossoms, of trees taking leaf and greenness, to turn thought kindly and thankfully; for ever beside you there is bloom, and ever beside you there is fruit, for which eye, heart, and soul are full of unknown and unspoken, because unspeakable, thank-offering.

And if sickness catches you, binds you, lays you down: no lonely moanings, and wicked curses at careless stepping nurses. *The* step is noiseless, and yet distinct beside you. The white curtains are drawn, or withdrawn, by the magic of that other presence; and the soft, cool hand is upon your brow.

No cold comfortings of friend-watchers, merely come

in to steal a word away from that outer world which is pulling at their skirts; but, ever, the sad, shaded brow of her, whose lightest sorrow for your sake is your greatest grief, if it were not a greater joy.

The blaze was leaping light and high, and the wood falling under the growing heat.

—— So, continued I, this heart would be at length itself; striving with everything gross, even now as it clings to grossness. Love would make its strength native and progressive. Earth's cares would fly. Joys would double. Susceptibilities be quickened; Love master self; and having made the mastery, stretch onward, and upward toward Infinitude.

And if the end came, and sickness brought that follower — Great Follower — which sooner or later is sure to come after, then the heart, and the hand of Love, ever near, are giving to your tired soul, daily and hourly, lessons of that love which consoles, which triumphs, which circleth all, and centreth in all, — Love Infinite and Divine!

Kind hands — none but *hers* — will smooth the hair upon your brow as the chill grows damp and heavy on it; and her fingers — none but hers — will lie in yours as the wasted flesh stiffens, and hardens for the ground. *Her* tears — you could feel no others, if oceans fell — will warm your drooping features once more to life; once more your eye, lighted in joyous triumph, kindle in her smile, and then —

The fire fell upon the hearth; the blaze gave a last leap, a flicker, then another, caught a little remaining twig, blazed up, wavered, went out.

There was nothing but a bed of glowing embers, over which the white ashes gathered fast. I was alone, with only my dog for company.

III.

Ashes — Signifying Desolation.

AFTER all, thought I, ashes follow blaze, inevitably as Death follows Life. Misery treads on the heels of Joy; Anguish rides swift after Pleasure.

"Come to me again, Carlo," said I to my dog; and I patted him fondly once more, but now only by the light of the dying embers.

It is very little pleasure one takes in fondling brute favorites; but it is a pleasure that when it passes leaves no void. It is only a little alleviating redundance in your solitary heart-life, which, if lost, another can be supplied.

But if your heart — not solitary, not quieting its humors with mere love of chase or dog, not repressing year after year its earnest yearnings after something better and more spiritual — has fairly linked itself by bonds strong as life to another heart, is the casting off easy, then?

Is it then only a little heart-redundancy cut off which the next bright sunset will fill up?

And my fancy, as it had painted doubt under the smoke, and cheer under warmth of the blaze, so now it began, under the faint light of the smouldering embers, to picture heart-desolation.

——What kind, congratulatory letters, hosts of them, coming from old and half-forgotten friends, now that your happiness is a year, or two years old!

"Beautiful."

——Aye, to be sure beautiful!

"Rich."

——Pho, the dawdler! how little he knows of heart-treasure who speaks of wealth to a man who loves his wife as a wife only should be loved!

"Young."

——Young indeed; guileless as infancy; charming as the morning.

Ah, these letters bear a sting: they bring to mind, with new and newer freshness, if it be possible, the value of that which you tremble lest you lose.

How anxiously you watch that step, if it lose not its buoyancy; how you study the color on that cheek, if it grow not fainter; how you tremble at the lustre in those eyes, if it be not the lustre of Death; how you totter under the weight of that muslin sleeve — a phantom weight! How you fear to do it, and yet press forward, to note if that breathing be quickened, as you ascend the home-heights, to look off on sunset lighting the plain.

Is your sleep quiet sleep, after that she has whispered to you her fears, and in the same breath — soft as a sigh, sharp as an arrow — bid you bear it bravely?

Perhaps — the embers were now glowing fresher, a little kindling, before the ashes — she triumphs over disease.

But Poverty, the world's almoner, has come to you with ready, spare hand.

Alone, with your dog living on bones, and you on hope — kindling each morning, dying slowly each night, — this could be borne. Philosophy would bring home its stores to the lone man. Money is not in his hand, but Knowledge is in his brain! and from that brain he draws out faster, as he draws slower from his pocket. He remembers: and on remembrance he can live for days, and weeks. The garret, if a garret covers him, is rich in fancies. The rain, if it pelts, pelts only him used to rain-peltings. And his dog crouches not in dread, but in companionship. His crust he divides with him, and laughs. He crowns himself with glorious memories of Cervantes, though he begs: if he nights it under the stars, he dreams heaven-sent dreams of the prisoned and homeless Galileo.

He hums old sonnets, and snatches of poor Jonson's plays. He chants Dryden's odes, and dwells on Otway's rhyme. He reasons with Bolingbroke or Diogenes, as the humor takes him; and laughs at the world: for the world, thank Heaven, has left him alone!

Keep your money, old misers, and your palaces. old princes, — the world is mine!

> " I care not, Fortune, what you me deny.
> You cannot rob me of free nature's grace,
> You cannot shut the windows of the sky,
> Through which Aurora shows her brightening face;
> You cannot bar my constant feet to trace
> The woods and lawns, by living streams, at eve.
> Let health my nerves and finer fibres brace,
> And I their toys to the great children leave:
> Of Fancy, Reason, Virtue, naught can me bereave!"

But — if not alone?

If *she* is clinging to you for support, for consolation, for home, for life, — she, reared in luxury perhaps, is faint for bread?

Then, the iron enters the soul; then the nights darken under any sky-light. Then the days grow long, even in the solstice of winter.

She may not complain; what then?

Will your heart grow strong, if the strength of her love can dam up the fountains of tears, and the tied tongue not tell of bereavement? Will it solace you to find her parting the poor treasure of food you have stolen for her, with begging, foodless children?

But this ill, strong hands, and Heaven's help, will put down. Wealth again; Flowers again; Patrimonial acres again; Brightness again. But your little Bessy, your favorite child, is pining.

Would to God! you say in agony, that wealth could

bring fulness again into that blanched cheek, or round those little thin lips once more; but it cannot. Thinner and thinner they grow; plaintive and more plaintive her sweet voice.

"Dear Bessy"—and your tones tremble; you feel that she is on the edge of the grave? Can you pluck her back? Can endearments stay her? Business is heavy, away from the loved child; home you go, to fondle while yet time is left; but *this* time you are too late. She is gone. She cannot hear you: she cannot thank you for the violets you put within her stiff white hand.

And then — the grassy mound — the cold shadow of the headstone!

The wind, growing with the night, is rattling at the window-panes, and whistles dismally. I wipe a tear and, in the interval of my Reverie, thank God that I am no such mourner.

But gayety, snail-footed, creeps back to the household. All is bright again; —

the violet bed's not sweeter
Than the delicious breath marriage sends forth.

Her lip is rich and full; her cheek delicate as a flower. Her frailty doubles your love.

And the little one she clasps — frail too — too frail the boy you had set your hopes and heart on. You have watched him growing, ever prettier, ever winning more and more upon your soul. The love you bore to him when he first lisped names — your name and hers — has doubled in strength, now that he asks innocently to be taught of this or that, and promises you, by that quick curiosity that flashes in his eye, a mind full of ntelligence.

And some hair-breadth escape by sea or flood, that he perhaps may have had, — which unstrung your soul to such tears as you pray God may be spared you again, — has endeared the little fellow to your heart a thousand-fold.

And now, with his pale sister in the grave, all *that* love has come away from the mound, where worms feast, and centres on the boy.

How you watch the storms lest they harm him! How often you steal to his bed late at night, and lay your hand lightly upon the brow, where the curls cluster thick, rising and falling with the throbbing temples, and watch, for minutes together, the little lips half parted, and listen — your ear close to them — if the breathing be regular and sweet!

But the day comes — the night rather — when you can catch no breathing.

Aye, put your hair away; compose yourself; listen again.

No, there is nothing!

Put your hand now to his brow, — damp, indeed,

but not with healthful night-sleep; it is not your hand,—no, do not deceive yourself,—it is your loved boy's forehead that is so cold; and your loved boy will never speak to you again—never play again—he is dead!

Oh, the tears—the tears; what blessed things are tears! Never fear now to let them fall on his forehead, or his lip, lest you waken him! Clasp him—clasp him harder; you cannot hurt, you cannot waken him! Lay him down, gently or not, it is the same; he is stiff; he is stark and cold.

But courage is elastic; it is our pride. It recovers itself easier, thought I, than these embers will get into blaze again.

But courage, and patience, and faith, and hope have their limit. Blessed be the man who escapes such trial as will determine limit!

To a lone man it comes not near; for how can trial take hold where there is nothing by which to try?

A funeral? You reason with philosophy. A graveyard? You read Hervey, and muse upon the wall. A friend dies? You sigh, you pat your dog; it is over. Losses? You retrench; you light your pipe; it is forgotten. Calumny? You laugh—you sleep.

But with that childless wife clinging to you in love and sorrow—what then?

Can you take down Seneca now, and coolly blow the dust from the leaf-tops? Can you crimp your lip with

Voltaire? Can you smoke idly, your feet dangling with the ivies, your thoughts all waving fancies upon a churchyard wall,—a wall that borders the grave of your boy?

Can you amuse yourself by turning stinging Martial into rhyme? Can you pat your dog, and seeing him wakeful and kind, say "It is enough"? Can you sneer at calumny, and sit by your fire dozing?

Blessed, thought I again, is the man who escapes such trial as will measure the limit of patience and the limit of courage!

But the trial comes: colder and colder were growing the embers.

That wife, over whom your love broods, is fading. Not beauty fading; that, now that your heart is wrapped in her being, would be nothing.

She sees with quick eye your dawning apprehension, and she tries hard to make that step of hers elastic.

Your trials and your loves together have centred your affections. They are not now as when you were a lone man, widespread and superficial. They have caught from domestic attachments a finer tone and touch. They cannot shoot out tendrils into barren world-soil, and suck up thence strengthening nutriment. They have grown under the forcing-glass of home-roof; they will not now bear exposure.

You do not now look men in the face as if a heart

ASHES — SIGNIFYING DESOLATION. 45

bond was linking you — as if a community of feeling lay between. There is a heart-bond that absorbs all others; there is a community that monopolizes your feeling. When the heart lay wide open, before it had grown upon and closed around particular objects, it could take strength and cheer from a hundred connections that now seem colder than ice.

And now those particular objects, alas for you! **are** failing.

What anxiety pursues you! How you struggle to fancy there is no danger; how she struggles to persuade you there is no danger!

How it grates now on your ear — the toil and turmoil of the city! It was music when you were alone; it was pleasant even, when from the din you were elaborating comforts for the cherished objects, — when you had such sweet escape as evening drew on.

Now it maddens you to see the world careless while you are steeped in care. They hustle you in the street; they smile at you across the table; they bow carelessly over the way; they do not know what canker is at your heart.

The undertaker comes with his bill for the dead boy's funeral. He knows your grief; he is respectful. You bless him in your soul. You wish the laughing street-goers were all undertakers.

Your eye follows the physician as he leaves you

house: is he wise? you ask yourself; is he prudent? is he the best? Did he never fail; is he never forgetful?

And now the hand that touches yours — is it no thinner, no whiter than yesterday? Sunny days come when he revives; color comes back; she breathes freer; she picks flowers; she meets you with a smile: hope lives again.

But the next day of storm she is fallen. She cannot talk even; she presses your hand.

You hurry away from business before your time. What matter for clients; who is to reap the rewards? What matter for fame; whose eye will it brighten? What matter for riches; whose is the inheritance?

You find her propped with pillows; she is looking over a little picture-book bethumbed by the dear boy she has lost. She hides it in her chair; she has pity on you.

——— Another day of revival, when the spring sun shines, and flowers open out-of-doors; she leans on your arm, and strolls into the garden where the first birds are singing. Listen to them with her; what memories are in bird-songs! You need not shudder at her tears; they are tears of Thanksgiving. Press the hand that lies light upon your arm, and you, too, thank God, while yet you may!

You are early home, mid-afternoon. Your step is not light; it is heavy, terrible.

ASHES — SIGNIFYING DESOLATION.

They have sent for you.

She is lying down, her eyes half closed, her breathing ong and interrupted.

She hears you; her eye opens; you put your hand in hers; yours trembles; hers does not. Her lips move; it is your name.

"Be strong," she says; "God will help you."

She presses harder your hand: "Adieu!"

A long breath, — another; you are alone again. No tears now; poor man! You cannot find them!

— — Again home early. There is a smell of varnish in your house. A coffin is there; they have clothed the body in decent grave-clothes, and the undertaker is screwing down the lid, slipping round on tiptoe. Does he fear to waken her?

He asks you a simple question about the inscription upon the plate, rubbing it with his coat-cuff. You look him straight in the eye; you motion to the door; you dare not speak.

He takes up his hat, and glides out stealthful as a cat.

The man has done his work well for all. It is a nice coffin, a very nice coffin. Pass your hand over it; how smooth!

Some sprigs of mignonette are lying carelessly in a little gilt-edged saucer. She loved mignonette.

It is a good stanch table the coffin rests on; it is *our* table; you are a housekeeper, a man of family

Aye, of family! keep down outcry, or the nurse will be in. Look over at the pinched features; is this all that is left of her? And where is your heart now? No, don't thrust your nails into your hands, nor mangle your lip, nor grate your teeth together. If you could only weep!

—— Another day. The coffin is gone out. The stupid mourners have wept — what idle tears! She with your crushed heart, has gone out.

Will you have pleasant evenings at your home now?

Go into your parlor that your prim housekeeper has made comfortable with clean hearth and blaze of sticks.

Sit down in your chair; there is another velvet-cushioned one, over against yours, empty. You press your fingers on your eyeballs, as if you would press out something that hurt the brain; but you cannot. Your head leans upon your hand; your eye rests upon the flashing blaze.

Ashes always come after blaze.

Go now into the room where she was sick, — softly, lest the prim housekeeper come after.

They have put new dimity upon her chair; they have hung new curtains over the bed. They have removed from the stand its phials, and silver bell; they have put a little vase of flowers in their place; the perfume will not offend the sick sense now. They have half opened the window, that the room so long closed may have air. It will not be too cold.

She is not there.

—— Oh God! thou who dost temper the wind to the shorn lamb, be kind!

The embers were dark; I stirred them; there was no sign of life. My dog was asleep. The clock in my tenant's chamber had struck one.

I dashed a tear or two from my eyes; how they came there I know not. I half ejaculated a prayer of thanks that such desolation had not yet come nigh me, and a prayer of hope that it might never come.

In a half hour more I was sleeping soundly. My reverie was ended.

SECOND REVERIE.

SEA-COAL AND ANTHRACITE.

BY A CITY GRATE.

BLESSED be letters!—they are the monitors, they are also the comforters, and they are the only true heart-talkers! Your speech, and their speeches, are conventional; they are moulded by circumstance; they are suggested by the observation, remark, and influence of the parties to whom the speaking is addressed, or by whom it may be overheard.

Your truest thought is modified half through its utterance by a look, a sign, a smile, or a sneer. It is not individual; it is not integral: it is social and mixed,— half of you, and half of others. It bends, it sways, it multiplies, it retires, and it advances, as the talk of others presses, relaxes, or quickens.

But it is not so of Letters. There you are, with only the soulless pen, and the snow-white, virgin paper. Your soul is measuring itself by itself, and saying its own sayings: there are no sneers to modify its utterance,— no scowl to scare; nothing is present but you and your thought.

Utter it then freely; write it down; stamp it; burn it in the ink!— There it is, a true soul-print!

Oh, the glory, the freedom, the passion of a letter! It is worth all the lip-talk in the world. Do you say, it is studied, made up, acted, rehearsed, contrived, artistic?

Let me see it then; let me run it over; tell me age, sex, circumstance, and I will tell you if it be studied or real,—if it be the merest lip-slang put into words, or heart-talk blazing on the paper.

I have a little packet, not very large, tied up with narrow crimson ribbon, now soiled with frequent handling, which far into some winter's night I take down from its nook upon my shelf, and untie, and open, and run over, with such sorrow and such joy, such tears and such smiles, as I am sure make me for weeks after a kinder and holier man.

There are in this little packet, letters in the familiar hand of a mother;— what gentle admonition; what tender affection! God have mercy on him who outlives the tears that such admonitions and such affection call up to the eye! There are others in the budget, in the delicate and unformed hand of a loved and lost sister,— written when she and you were full of glee, and the best mirth of youthfulness; does it harm you to recall that mirthfulness? or to trace again, for the hundredth time, that scrawling postscript at the bottom, with its *i*'s so carefully dotted, and its gigantic *t*'s so carefully crossed, by the childish hand of a little brother?

I have added latterly to that packet of letters. I almost need a new and longer ribbon; the old one is getting too short. Not a few of these new and cherished letters a former Reverie* has brought to me; not letters of cold praise, saying it was well done, artfully executed, prettily imagined; no such thing: but letters of sympathy — of sympathy which means sympathy — the παθήμί and the συν.

It would be cold and dastardly work to copy them; I am too selfish for that. It is enough to say that they, the kind writers, have seen a heart in the Reverie, — have felt that it was real, true. They know it; a secret influence has told it. What matters it, pray, if literally there was no wife, and no dead child, and no coffin, in the house? Is not feeling, feeling; and heart, heart? Are not these fancies thronging on my brain, bringing tears to my eyes, bringing joy to my soul, as living as anything human can be living? What if they have no material type — no objective form? All that is crude — a mere reduction of ideality to sense, — a transformation of the spiritual to the earthy, — a levelling of soul to matter.

---

* The first Reverie — Smoke, Flame, and Ashes — was published some months previous to this, in the *Southern Literary Messenger*.

Are we not creatures of thought and passion? Is anything about us more earnest than that same thought and passion? Is there anything more real,— more characteristic of that great and dim destiny to which we are born, and which may be written down in that terrible word— Forever?

Let those who will, then, sneer at what in their wisdom they call untruth,— at what is false, because it has no material presence: this does not create falsity; would to Heaven that it did!

And yet, if there was actual, material truth, super added to Reverie, would such objectors sympathize the more? No! a thousand times, no; the heart that has no sympathy with thoughts and feelings that scorch the soul, is dead also — whatever its mocking tears and gestures may say — to a coffin or a grave!

Let them pass, and we will come back to these cherished letters.

A mother, who has lost a child, has, she says, shed a tear — not one, but many — over the dead boy's coldness. And another, who has not lost, but who trembles lest she lose, has found the words failing as she read, and a dim, sorrow-borne mist spreading over the page.

Another, yet rejoicing in all those family ties that make life a charm, has listened nervously to careful reading, until the husband is called home, and the coffin is in the house. "Stop!" she says; and a gush of tears tells the rest.

Yet the cold critic will say, "It was artfully done." A curse on him! it was not art: it was nature.

Another, a young, fresh, healthful girl-mind, has seen something in the love-picture — albeit so weak — of truth; and has kindly believed that it must be earnest. Aye, indeed is it, fair and generous one, earnest as life and hope! Who, indeed, with a heart at all, that has not yet slipped away irreparably and forever from the shores of youth, — from that fairy land which young enthusiasm creates, and over which bright dreams hover, — but knows it to be real? And so such things will be real till hopes are dashed, and Death is come.

Another, a father, has laid down the book in tears.

— God bless them all! How far better this than the cold praise of newspaper paragraphs, or the critically contrived approval of colder friends!

Let me gather up these letters carefully, to be read when the heart is faint and sick of all that there is unreal and selfish in the world. Let me tie them together with a new and longer bit of ribbon; not by a love-knot, that is too hard; but by an easy slipping knot, that so I may get at them the better. And now they are all together, a snug packet, and we will label them, not sentimentally (I pity the one who thinks it!) but earnestly, and in the best meaning of the term, — SOUVENIRS DU CŒUR.

Thanks to my first Reverie, which has added to such a treasure!

—And now to my SECOND REVERIE.

I am no longer in the country. The fields, the trees, the brooks are far away from me, and yet they are very present. A letter from my tenant—how different from those other letters!—lies upon my table, telling me what fields he has broken up for the autumn grain, and how many beeves he is fattening, and how the potatoes are turning out.

But I am in a garret of the city. From my window I look over a mass of crowded house-tops,—moralizing often upon the scene, but in a strain too long and sombre to be set down here. In place of the wide country chimney, with its iron fire-dogs, is a snug grate, where the maid makes me a fire in the morning, and rekindles it in the afternoon.

I am usually fairly seated in my chair—a cosily stuffed office-chair—by five or six o'clock of the evening. The fire has been newly made, perhaps an hour before: first, the maid drops a withe of paper in the bottom of the grate, then a stick or two of pine-wood, and after it a hod of Liverpool coal; so that by the time I am seated for the evening, the sea-coal is fairly in a blaze.

When this has sunk to a level with the second bar of the grate, the maid replenishes it with a hod of Anthracite; and I sit musing and reading, while the new coal warms and kindles; not leaving my place, until it has sunk to the third bar of the grate, which marks my bedtime.

I love these accidental measures of the hours, which belong to you, and your life, and not to the world. A watch is no more the measure of your time than of the time of your neighbors; a church-clock is as public and vulgar as a church-warden. I would as soon think of hiring the parish sexton to make my bed, as to regulate my time by the parish clock.

A shadow that the sun casts upon your carpet, or a streak of light on a slated roof yonder, or the burning of your fire, are pleasant time-keepers, — full of presence, full of companionship, and full of the warning — time is passing!

In the summer season I have even measured my reading, and my night-watch, by the burning of a taper; and I have scratched upon the handle to the little bronze taper-holder that meaning passage of the New Testament, — Νυξ γαρ ερχεται, — the night cometh!

But I must get upon my Reverie. It was a drizzly evening; I had worked hard during the day, and had drawn my boots, thrust my feet into slippers, thrown on a Turkish loose dress and Greek cap, souvenirs to me of other times and other places, — and sat watching the lively, uncertain, yellow play of the bituminous flame.

L.

Sea-Coal.

IT is like a flirt, mused I: lively, uncertain, bright, colored, waving here and there, melting the coal into black, shapeless mass; making foul, sooty smoke, and pasty, trashy residuum! Yet withal, pleasantly sparkling, dancing, prettily waving, and leaping like a roebuck from point to point.

How like a flirt! And yet is not this tossing caprice of girlhood, to which I liken my sea-coal flame, a native play of life, and belonging by nature to the playtime of life? Is it not a sort of essential fire-kindling to the weightier and truer passions, even as Jenny puts the soft coal first, the better to kindle the anthracite? Is it not a sort of necessary consumption of young vapors, which float in the soul, and which is left thereafter the purer? Is there not a stage somewhere in every man's youth for just such waving, idle heartblaze, which means nothing, yet which must be got over?

Lamartine says somewhere, very prettily, that there is more of quick-running sap and floating shade in a young tree, but more of fire in the heart of a sturdy oak:—' *Il y a plus de sève folle et d'ombre flottante dans les jeunes plants de la forêt ; il y a plus de feu dans le vieux cœur du chêne.*"

Is Lamartine playing off his prettiness of expression dressing up with his poetry,—making a good conscience against the ghost of some accusing Graziella,— or is there truth in the matter?

A man who has seen sixty years, whether widower or bachelor, may well put such sentiment into words : it feeds his wasted heart with hope ; it renews the exultation of youth by the pleasantest of equivocation, and the most charming of self-confidence. But, after all, is it not true? Is not the heart like new blossoming field-plants, whose first flowers are half-formed, one-sided perhaps, but by-and-by, in maturity of season, putting out wholesome, well-formed blossoms, that will hold their leaves long and bravely?

Bulwer, in his story of the Caxtons, has counted first heart-flights mere fancy passages,—a dalliance with the breezes of love,— which pass, and leave healthful heart-appetite. Half the reading world has read the story of Trevanion and Pisistratus. But Bulwer is—past his heart-life is used up—*épuisé.* Such a man can very safely rant about the cool judgment of after-years.

Where does Shakspeare put the unripe heart-age? All of it before the ambition, that alone makes the hero-soul. The Shakspeare man "sighs like a furnace," before he stretches his arm to achieve the "bauble, reputation."

Yet Shakspeare has meted a soul-love, mature and ripe, without any young furnace-sighs, to Desdemona and Othello. Cordelia, the sweetest of his play-creations, loves without any of the mawkish matter which makes the whining love of a Juliet. And Florizel, in the "Winter's Tale," says to Perdita, in the true spirit of a most sound heart,—

> "My desires
> Run not before mine honor, nor my lusts
> Burn hotter than my faith."

How is it with Hector and Andromache? No sea-coal blaze, but one that is constant, enduring, pervading: a pair of hearts full of esteem and best love,—good, honest, and sound.

Look now at Adam and Eve, in God's presence, with Milton for showman. Shall we quote by this sparkling blaze, a gem from the "Paradise Lost"? We will hum it to ourselves,—what Raphael sings to Adam,—a classic song:—

> " Him, serve and fear!
> Of other creatures, as Him pleases best
> Wherever placed, let Him dispose; joy thou
> In what he gives to thee, this Paradise
> And thy fair Eve!"

And again : —
> " Love refines
> The thoughts and heart enlarges: hath his seat
> In reason, and is judicious: is the scale
> By which to Heavenly love thou mayst ascend ! "

None of the playing sparkle in this love, which belongs to the flame of my sea-coal fire, that is now dancing, lively as a cricket. But on looking about my garret-chamber, I can see nothing that resembles the archangel Raphael, or "thy fair Eve."

There is a degree of moisture about the sea-coal flame, which, with the most earnest of my musing, I find it impossible to attach to that idea of a waving, sparkling heart which my fire suggests. A damp heart must be a foul thing to be sure! But whoever heard of one?

Wordsworth, somewhere in the " Excursion," says : —
> " The good die first,
> And they whose hearts are *dry* as summer dust
> Burn to the socket ! "

What, in the name of Rydal Mount, is a dry heart? A dusty one, I can conceive of: a bachelor's heart must be somewhat dusty, as he nears the sixtieth summer of his pilgrimage ; and hung over with cobwebs, in which sit such watchful gray old spiders as Avarice and Selfishness, forever on the look-out for such bottle green flies as Lust.

" I will never," said I, griping at the elbows of my

chair, "live a bachelor till sixty: never, so surely as there is hope in man, or charity in woman, or faith in both!"

And with that thought, my heart leaped about in playful coruscations, even like the flame of the sea-coal: rising and wrapping round old and tender memories, and images that were present to me, trying to cling, and yet no sooner fastened than off; dancing again, riotous in its exultation, — a succession of heart-sparkles, blazing, and going out!

— And is there not, mused I, a portion of this world forever blazing in just such lively sparkles, waving here and there as the air-currents fan them?

Take, for instance, your heart of sentiment and quick sensibility, — a weak, warm-working heart, flying off in tangents of unhappy influence, unguided by prudence, and perhaps virtue. There is a paper by Mackenzie in the *Mirror* for April, 1780, which sets this untoward sensibility in a strong light.

And the more it is indulged, the more strong and binding such a habit of sensibility becomes. Poor Mackenzie himself must have suffered thus; you cannot read his books without feeling it; your eye, in spit of you, runs over with his sensitive griefs, while you are half ashamed of his success at picture-making. It is a terrible inheritance, and one that a strong man or woman will study to subdue; it is a vain sea-coal spark ling, which will count no good. The world is made of much hard, flinty substance, against which your better and holier thoughts will be striking fire : see to it that the sparks do not burn you!

But what a happy careless life belongs to this Bachelorhood, in which you may strike out boldly right and eft! Your heart is not bound to another which may be full of only sickly vapors of feeling; nor is it frozen to a cold man's heart under a silk bodice, knowing nothing of tenderness but the name, to prate of; and nothing of soul-confidence, but clumsy confession. And if, in your careless out-goings of feeling, you get here only a little lip vapidity in return, be sure that you will find elsewhere a true heart utterance. This last you will cherish in your inner soul, a nucleus for a new group of affections; and the other will pass with a whiff of your cigar.

Or if your feelings are touched, struck, hurt, who is the wiser, or the worse, but you only? And have you not the whole skein of your heart-life in your own fingers, to wind or unwind in what shape you please? Shake it, or twine it, or tangle it, by the light of your fire, as you fancy best. He is a weak man who canno twist and weave the threads of his feeling — howevei fine, however tangled, however strained, or however strong — into the great cable of Purpose, by which he lies moored to his life of Action.

Reading is a great and happy disentangler of all those knotted snarls — those extravagant vagaries, which belong to a heart sparkling with sensibility; but the reading must be cautiously directed. There is old, placid Burton, when your soul is weak and its digestion of life's humors is bad; there is Cowper, when your spirit runs into kindly, half-sad, religious musing there is Crabbe, when you would shake off vagary, by a little handling of sharp actualities. There is Voltaire, a homœopathic doctor, whom you can read when you want to make a play of life, and crack jokes at Nature, and be witty with Destiny; there is Rousseau, when you want to lose yourself in a mental dream-land, and be beguiled by the harmony of soul-music and soul-culture.

And when you would shake off this, and be sturdiest among the battlers for hard world-success, and be forewarned of rocks against which you must surely smite, — read Bolingbroke; run over the letters of Lyttleton; read, and think of what you read, in the cracking lines of Rochefoucauld. How he sums us up in his stinging words! how he puts the scalpel between the crves! yet he never hurts, for he is dissecting dead natter.

If you are in a genial, careless mood, who is better than such extemporizers of feeling and nature — good-hearted fellows — as Sterne and Fielding?

And then again, there are Milton and Isaiah, to lift up one's soul until it touches cloud-land, and you wander with their guidance, on swift feet, to the very gates of heaven.

But this sparkling sensibility to one struggling under infirmity, or with grief or poverty, is very dreadful. The soul is too nicely and keenly hinged to be wrenched without mischief. How it shrinks, like a hurt child, from all that is vulgar, harsh, and crude! Alas, for such a man! he will be buffeted from beginning to end; his life will be a sea of troubles. The poor victim of his own quick spirit, he wanders with a great shield of doubt hung before him, so that none, not even friends, can see the goodness of such kindly qualities as belong to him. Poverty, if it comes upon him, he wrestles with in secret, with strong, frenzied struggles. He wraps his scant clothes about him to keep him from the cold; and eyes the world as if every creature in it was breathing chill blasts at him from every opened mouth. He threads the crowded ways of the city, proud in his griefs, vain in his weakness, not stopping to do good. Bulwer, in the " New Timon," has painted, in a pair of stinging Pope-like lines, this feeling in a woman : —

> " What had been pride, a kind of madness grown,
> She hugged her wrongs, her sorrow was her throne! "

Cold picture! yet the heart was sparkling under it.

like my sea-coal fire, — lifting and blazing, and lighting and falling, — but with no object, and only such little heat as begins and ends within.

Those fine sensibilities, ever active, are chasing and observing all; they catch a hue from what the dull and callous pass by unnoticed — because unknown. They blunder at the great variety of the world's opinions they see tokens of belief where others see none. That delicate organization is a curse to a man; and yet, poor fool, he does not see where his cure lies; he wonders at his griefs, and has never reckoned with himself their source. He studies others, without studying himself. He eats the leaves that sicken, and never plucks up the root that will cure.

With a woman it is worse: with her, this delicate susceptibility is like a frail flower, that quivers at every rough blast of heaven; her own delicacy wounds her; her highest charm is perverted to a curse.

She listens with fear; she reads with trembling; she looks with dread. Her sympathies give a tone, like the harp of Æolus, to the slightest breath. Her sensibility ights up, and quivers and falls, like the flame of a sea-oal fire.

If she loves, (and may not a Bachelor reason on nis daintiest of topics,) her love is a gushing, wavy flame, lit up with hope, that has only a little kindling matter to light it; and this soon burns out. Yet in tense sensibility will persuade her that the flame still scorches. She will mistake the annoyance of affection unrequited for the sting of a passion that she fancies still burns. She does not look deep enough to see that the passion is gone, and the shocked sensitiveness emits only faint, yellowish sparkles in its place; her high wrought organization makes those sparks seem a veritable flame.

With her, judgment, prudence, and discretion are cold, measured terms, which have no meaning, except as they attach to the actions of others. Of her own acts, she never predicates them; feeling is much too high, to allow her to submit to any such obtrusive guides of conduct. She needs disappointment to teach her truth,— to teach that all is not gold that glitters,— to teach that all warmth does not blaze. But let her beware how she sinks under any fancied disappointments: she who sinks under real disappointment lacks philosophy; but she who sinks under a fancied one lacks purpose. Let her flee as the plague such brooding thoughts as she will love to cherish; let her spurn dark fancies as the visitants of hell; let the soul rise with the blaze of new-kindled, active, and world-wide emotions, and so brighten into steady and constant flame. Let her abjure such poets as Cowper, or Byron, or even Wordsworth; and of she must poetize, let her lay her mind to such manly verse as Pope's, or to such sound and ringing organry as Comus.

My fire was getting dull, and I thrust in the poker It started up on the instant into a hundred little angry tongues of flame.

— Just so, thought I, the over-sensitive heart, once cruelly disturbed, will fling out a score of flaming passions, darting here and darting there, half smoke, half flame, — love and hate, canker and joy, — wild in its madness, not knowing whither its sparks are flying. Once break roughly upon the affections, or even the fancied affections of such a soul, and you breed a tornado of maddened action, — a whirlwind of fire that hisses, and sends out jets of wild, impulsive combustion, that make the bystanders, even those most friendly, stand aloof until the storm is past.

But this is not all that the dashing flame of my seacoal suggests.

———— How like a flirt! mused I again, recurring to my first thought: so lively, yet uncertain; so bright, yet so flickering! Your true flirt plays with sparkles; her heart, much as there is of it, spends itself in sparkles; she measures it to sparkle, and habit grows into nature, so that anon it can only sparkle. How carefully she cramps it, if the flames show too great a heat; how dexterously she flings its blaze here and there; how coyly she subdues it; how winningly she lights it!

All this is the entire reverse of the unpremeditated

dartings of the soul at which I have been looking; sensibility scorns heart-curbings and heart-teachings; sensibility inquires not, how much? but only, where?

Your true flirt has a coarse-grained soul; well modulated and well tutored, but there is no fineness in it. All its native fineness is made coarse by coarse efforts of the will. True feeling is a rustic vulgarity the flirt does not tolerate; she counts its healthiest and most honest manifestation all sentiment. Yet she will play you off a pretty string of sentiment which she has gathered from the poets; she adjusts it prettily as a Gobelin weaver adjusts the colors in his *tapis*. She shades it off delightfully; there are no bold contrasts, but a most artistic mellow of *nuances*.

She smiles like a wizard, and jingles it with a laugh, such as tolled the poor home-bound Ulysses to the Circean bower. She has a cast of the head, apt and artful as the most dexterous cast of the best trout-killing rod. Her words sparkle, and flow hurriedly, and with the prettiest doubleness of meaning. Naturalness she copies, and she scorns. She accuses herself of a single expression or regard, which nature prompts. She prides herself on her schooling. She measures her wit by the triumphs of her art; she chuckles over her own falsity to herself. And if by chance her soul — such germ as is left of it — betrays her into untoward confidence, she condemns herself, as if she had committed crime.

She is always gay, because she has no depth of feeling to be stirred. The brook that runs shallow over hard, pebbly bottom always rustles. She is light-hearted, because her heart floats in sparkles, like my sea-coal fire. She counts on marriage, not as the great absorbent of a heart's-love, and life, but as a happy, feasible, and orderly conventionality, to be played with, and kept at distance, and finally to be accepted as a cover for the faint and tawdry sparkles of an old and cherished heartlessness.

She will not pine under any regrets, because she has no appreciation of any loss; she will not chafe at indifference, because it is her art; she will not be worried with jealousies, because she is ignorant of love. With no conception of the soul in its strength and fulness, she sees no lack of its demands. A thrill she does not know; a passion she cannot imagine; joy is a name; grief is another; and Life, with its crowding scenes of love and bitterness, is a play upon the stage.

I think it is Madame Dudevant who says, in something like the same connection:—"*Les hiboux ne connaissent pas le chemin par où les aigles vont au soleil.*"

—— Poor Ned! mused I, looking at the play of the fire, was a victim and a conqueror. He was a man of a full, strong nature,—not a little impulsive,—with action too full of earnestness for most of men to see its drift. He had known little of what is called the world: he was fresh in feeling and high of hope; he had been encircled always by friends who loved him, and who, maybe, flattered him. Scarce had he entered upon the tangled life of the city, before he met with a sparkling face and an airy step, that stirred something in poor Ned that he had never felt before. With him, to feel was to act. He was not one to be despised; for notwithstanding he wore a country air, and the awkwardness of a man who has yet the *bienséance* of social life before him, he had the soul, the courage, and the talent of a strong man. Little gifted in the knowledge of face-play, he easily mistook those coy manœuvres of a sparkling heart for something kindred to his own true emotions.

She was proud of the attentions of a man who carried a mind in his brain, and flattered poor Ned almost into servility. Ned had no friends to counsel him; or if he had them, his impulses would have blinded him. Never was dodger more artful at the Olympic Games than the Peggy of Ned's heart-affection. He was charmed, beguiled, entranced.

When Ned spoke of love, she staved it off with the prettiest of sly looks that only bewildered him the more. A charming creature to be sure; coy as a dove

So he went on, poor fool, until one day — he told me of it with the blood mounting to his temples, and his eye shooting flame — he suffered his feelings to run out in passionate avowal, — entreaty, — everything. She gave a pleasant, noisy laugh, and manifested — such pretty surprise!

He was looking for the intense glow of passion; and lo! there was nothing but the shifting sparkle of a sea-coal flame.

I wrote him a letter of condolence, for I was his senior by a year. "My dear fellow," said I, "diet yourself: you can find greens at the up-town market; eat a little fish with your dinner; abstain from heating drinks; don't put too much butter to your cauliflower; read one of Jeremy Taylor's sermons, and translate all the quotations at sight; run carefully over that exquisite picture of Geo. Dandin in your Molière, and my word for it, in a week you will be a sound man."

He was too angry to reply; but eighteen months thereafter I got a thick, three-sheeted letter, with a dove upon the seal, telling me that he was as happy as a king. He said he had married a good-hearted, domestic, loving wife, who was as lovely as a June-day; and that their baby, not three months old, was as bright as a spot of June-day sunshine on the grass.

— What a tender, delicate, loving wife, mused I, such flashing, flaming flirt must in the end make; — the prostitute of fashion; the bauble of fifty hearts idle as hers; the shifting makepeace of a stage-scene; the actress, now in peasant, and now in princely petticoats!

How it would cheer an honest soul to call her — his. What a culmination of his heart-life; what a rich dream-land to be realized!

―― Bah! and I thrust the poker into the clotted mass of fading coal; just such, and so worthless, is the used heart of a city flirt; just so the incessant sparkle of her life, and frittering passions, fuses all that is sound and combustible into black, sooty, shapeless residuum.

When I marry a flirt, I will buy second-hand clothes of the Jews.

— Still, mused I, as the flame danced again, there is a distinction between coquetry and flirtation.

A coquette sparkles, but it is more the sparkle of a harmless and pretty vanity than of calculation. It is the play of humors in the blood, and not the play of purpose at the heart. It will flicker around a true soul like the blaze around an *omelette au rhum*, leaving the kernel sounder and warmer.

Coquetry, with all its pranks and teasings, makes the spice to your dinner — the mulled wine to your supper. It will drive you to desperation, only to bring you back hotter to the fray. Who would boast a victory that cost no strategy, and no careful disposition of the forces? Who would bulletin such success as my Uncle Toby's, in a back-garden, with only the Corporal Trim for assailant? But let a man be very sure that the city is worth the siege!

Coquetry whets the appetite; flirtation depraves it Coquetry is the thorn that guards the rose, — easily trimmed off when once plucked. Flirtation is like the slime on water-plants, making them hard to handle, and when caught, only to be cherished in slimy waters.

And so, with my eye clinging to the flickering blaze I see in my reverie a bright one dancing before me with sparkling, coquettish smile, teasing me with the prettiest graces in the world; and I grow maddened between hope and fear, and still watch with my whole soul in my eyes; and see her features by-and-by relax to pity, as a gleam of sensibility comes stealing over her spirit; and then to a kindly, feeling regard: presently she approaches, — a coy and doubtful approach, — and throws back the ringlets that lie over her cheek, and lays her hand — a little bit of white hand — timidly upon my strong fingers, and turns her head daintily to one side, and looks up in my eyes as they rest on the playing blaze; and my fingers close fast and passionately over that little hand, like a swift night-cloud shrouding the pale tips of Dian; and my eyes draw nearer and nearer to those blue, laughing, pitying, teasing eyes, and my arm clasps round that shadowy form, — and my lips feel a warm breath — growing warmer and warmer ——

Just here the maid comes in, and throws upon the fire a panful of Anthracite, and my sparkling sea-coal reverie is ended.

II.

Anthracite.

IT does not burn freely, so I put on the blower. Quaint and good-natured Xavier de Maistre * would have made, I dare say, a pretty epilogue about a sheet-iron blower; but I cannot.

I try to bring back the image that belonged to the lingering bituminous flame, but with my eyes on that dark blower — how can I?

It is the black curtain of destiny which drops down before our brightest dreams. How often the phantoms of joy regale us, and dance before us, golden-winged, angel-faced, heart-warming, and make an Elysium in which the dreaming soul bathes, and feels translated to another existence; and then — sudden as night, or a cloud — a word, a step, a thought, a memory will chase them away, like scared deer vanishing over a gray horizon of moor-land!

I know not justly, if it be a weakness or a sin to

* *Voyage autour de Ma Chambre.*

create these phantoms that we love, and to group them into a paradise — soul-created. But if it is a sin, it is a sweet and enchanting sin; and if it is a weakness, it is a strong and stirring weakness. If this heart is sick of the falsities that meet it at every hand, and is eager to spend that power which nature has ribbed it with on some object worthy of its fulness and depth, shall it not feel a rich relief, nay more, an exercise in keeping with its end, if it flow out, strong as a tempest, wild as a rushing river, upon those ideal creations which imagination invents, and which are tempered by our best sense of beauty, purity, and grace?

—— Useless, do you say? Aye, it is as useless as the pleasure of looking hour upon hour over bright landscapes · it is as useless as the rapt enjoyment of listening, with heart full and eyes brimming, to such music as the *Miserere* at Rome; it is as useless as the ecstasy of kindling your soul into fervor and love and madness, over pages that reek with genius.

There are indeed base-moulded souls who know nothing of this: they laugh; they sneer; they even affect to pity. Just so the Huns under the avenging Attila, who had been used to foul cookery and steaks stewed under their saddles, laughed brutally at the spiced banquets of an Apicius!

—— No, this phantom-making is no sin; or if it be, it is sinning with a soul so full, so earnest, that it can cry to Heaven cheerily, and sure of a gracious hearing, — *peccavi* — *misericorde!*

But my fire is in a glow, a pleasant glow, throwing a tranquil, steady light to the farthest corner of my garret. How unlike it is to the flashing play of the sea-coal! — unlike as an unsteady, uncertain-working heart to the true and earnest constancy of one cheerful and right.

After all, thought I, give me such a heart; not bent on vanities, not blazing too sharp with sensibility, not throwing out coquettish jets of flame, not wavering, and meaningless with pretended warmth, but open, glowing, and strong. Its dark shades and angles it may have; for what is a soul worth that does not take a slaty tinge from those griefs that chill the blood? Yet still the fire is gleaming; you see it in the crevices; and anon it will give radiance to the whole mass.

—— It hurts the eyes, this fire; and I draw up a screen painted over with rough but graceful figures.

The true heart wears always the veil of modesty, (not of prudery, which is a dingy, iron, repulsive screen.) It will not allow itself to be looked on too near, — it might scorch; but through the veil you feel the warmth and through the pretty figures that modesty will robe itself in, you can see all the while the golden outlines, and by that token you *know* that it is glowing and burning with a pure and steady flame.

With such a heart the mind fuses naturally,— a holy and heated fusion; they work together like twins-born. With such a heart, as Raphael says to Adam,

> " Love hath his seat
> In reason, and is judicious."

But let me distinguish this heart from your clay-cold, lukewarm, half-hearted soul;— considerate, because ignorant; judicious, because possessed of no latent fires that need a curb; prudish, because with no warm blood to tempt. This sort of soul may pass scatheless through the fiery furnace of life; strong only in its weakness; pure, because of its failings; and good only by negation. It may triumph over love, and sin, and death; but it will be a triumph of the beast, which has neither passions to subdue, or energy to attack, or hope to quench.

Let us come back to the steady and earnest heart, glowing like my anthracite coal.

I fancy I see such a one now;— the eye is deep, and reaches back to the spirit; it is not the trading eye, weighing your purse; it is not the worldly eye, weighing position; it is not the beastly eye, weighing your appearance; it is the heart's eye, weighing your soul!

It is full of deep, tender, and earnest feeling. It is an eye which, looked on once, you long to look on again it is an eye which will haunt your dreams,— an eye which will give a color, in spite of you, to all your reveries. It is an eye which lies before you in your future, like a star in the mariner's heaven; by it, unconsciously, and from force of deep soul-habit, you take all your observations. It is meek and quiet; but it is full, as a spring that gushes in flood; an Aphrodite and a Mercury — a Vaucluse and a Clitumnus.

The face is an angel face: no matter for curious lines of beauty; no matter for popular talk of prettiness; no matter for its angles or its proportions; no matter for its color or its form, — the soul is there, illuminating every feature, burnishing every point, hallowing every surface. It tells of honesty, sincerity, and worth; it tells of truth and virtue; — and you clasp the image to your heart, as the received ideal of your fondest dreams.

The figure may be this or that, it may be tall or short; it matters nothing, — the heart is there. The talk may be soft or low, serious or piquant, — a free and honest soul is warming and softening it all. As you speak, it speaks back again; as you think, it thinks again, (not in conjunction, but in the same sign of the Zodiac;) as you love, it loves in return.

—— It is the heart for a sister, and happy is the man who can claim such! The warmth that lies in it is not only generous, but religious, genial, devotional, tender self-sacrificing, and looking heavenward

A man without some sort of religion is at best a poor reprobate, the foot-ball of destiny, with no tie linking him to infinity and the wondrous eternity that is begun with him; but a woman without it is even worse,— a flame without heat, a rainbow without color, a flower without perfume!

A man may in some sort tie his frail hopes and honor with weak, shifting ground-tackle to business, or to the world; but a woman without that anchor which they call Faith, is adrift and a-wreck! A man may clumsily contrive a kind of moral responsibility out of his relations to mankind; but a woman in her comparatively isolated sphere, where affection and not purpose is the controlling motive, can find no basis for any system of right action but that of spiritual faith. A man may craze his thought and his brain to trustfulness in such poor harborage as Fame and Reputation may stretch before him; but a woman — where can she put her hope in storms, if not in Heaven?

And that sweet trustfulness, that abiding love, that enduring hope, mellowing every page and scene of life, lighting them with pleasantest radiance, when the world-storms break like an army with smoking cannon, — what can bestow it all but a holy soul-tie to what is above the storms, and to what is stronger than an army with cannon? Who that has enjoyed the counsel and the love of a Christian mother, but will echo the thought with energy, and hallow it with a tear? — *et noi, je pleurs!*

My fire is now a mass of red-hot coal. The whole atmosphere of my room is warm. The heart that with its glow can light up and warm a garret with loose casements and shattered roof, is capable of the best love, — domestic love. I draw farther off, and the images upon the screen change. The warmth, the hour, the quiet, create a home feeling; and that feeling, quick as lightning, has stolen from the world of fancy (a Promethean theft) a home object, about which my musings go on to drape themselves in luxurious reverie.

—— There she sits, by the corner of the fire, in a neat home dress of sober, yet most adorning color. A little bit of lace ruffle is gathered about the neck by a blue ribbon; and the ends of the ribbon are crossed under the dimpling chin, and are fastened neatly by a simple, unpretending brooch, — your gift. The arm, a pretty taper arm, lies over the carved elbow of the oaken chair; the hand, white and delicate, sustains a little home volume that hangs from her fingers. The forefinger is between the leaves, and the others lie in relief upon the dark embossed cover. She repeats, in a silver voice, a line that has attracted her fancy; and you listen, — or, at any rate, you seem to listen, — with your eyes now on the lips, now on the forehead, and now on the finger, where glitters like a star the marriage-ring — little gold band, at which she does not chafe — that tells you — she is yours !

—— Weak testimonial, if that were all that told it! The eye, the voice, the look, the heart, tells you stronger and better, that she is yours. And a feeling within, where it lies you know not, and whence it comes you know not, but sweeping over heart and brain like a fire-flood, tells you too, that you are hers! Irremediably bound as Hortensio in the play : —

> "I am subject to another's will, and can
> Nor speak, nor do, without permission from her!"

The fire is warm as ever : what length of heat in this hard burning anthracite! It has scarce sunk yet to the second bar of the grate, though the clock upon the church-tower has tolled eleven.

— Aye, mused I, gayly, such a heart does not grow faint, it does not spend itself in idle puffs of blaze, it does not become chilly with the passing years; but it gains and grows in strength and heat, until the fire of life is covered over with the ashes of death. Strong or hot as it may be at the first, it loses nothing. It may not, indeed, as time advances, throw out, like the coal-fire, when new-lit, jets of blue sparkling flame; it may not continue to bubble, and gush like a fountain at its source, but it will become a strong river of flowing charities.

Clitumnus breaks from under the Tuscan mountains, almost a flood. On a glorious spring day I leaned down and tasted the water, as it boiled from its sources. The little temple of white marble, the mountain sides gray with olive orchards, the white streak of road, the tall poplars of the river margin were glistening in the bright Italian sunlight around me. Later, I saw it when it had become a river, — still clear and strong, flowing serenely between its prairie banks, on which the white cattle of the valley browsed; and still farther down, I welcomed it, where it joins the Arno, — flowing slowly under wooded shores, skirting the fair Florence, and the bounteous fields of the bright Cascino, — gathering strength and volume, till between Pisa and Leghorn, in sight of the wondrous Leaning Tower, and the ship-masts of the Tuscan port, it gave its waters to its life's grave — the sea.

The recollection blended sweetly now with my musings over my garret-grate, and offered a flowing image, to bear along upon its bosom the affections that were grouping in my Reverie.

It is a strange force of the mind and of the fancy that can set the objects which are closest to the hear far down the lapse of time. Even now, as the fire fades slightly, and sinks slowly towards the bar, which is the dial of my hours, I seem to see that image of love which has played about the fire-glow of my grate, years hence

It still covers the same warm, trustful, religious heart Trials have tried it; afflictions have weighed upon it danger has scared it, and death is coming near to subdue it; but still it is the same.

The fingers are thinner; the face has lines of care and sorrow, crossing each other in a web-work that makes the golden tissue of humanity. But the heart is fond and steady; it is the same dear heart, the same self-sacrificing heart, warming, like a fire, all around it Affliction has tempered joy, and joy adorned affliction Life and all its troubles have become distilled into an holy incense, rising ever from your fireside — an offering to your household gods.

Your dreams of reputation, your swift determination, your impulsive pride, your deep-uttered vows to win a name, have all sobered into affection, — have all blended into that glow of feeling which finds its centre and hope and joy in HOME. From my soul I pity him whose soul does not leap at the mere utterance of that name.

A home! it is the bright, blessed, adorable phantom which sits highest on the sunny horizon that girdeth Life! When shall it be reached? When shall it cease to be a glittering day-dream, and become fully and fairly yours?

It is not the house, — though that may have its charms; nor the fields carefully tilled, and streaked with your own footpaths; nor the trees, — though their shadow be to you like that of a great rock in a weary land; nor yet is it the fireside, with its sweet blaze, play; nor the pictures which tell of loved ones; nor the cherished books; but more far than all these, — it is the PRESENCE. The *Lares* of your worship are there; the altar of your confidence is there; the end of your worldly faith is there; and adorning it all, and sending your blood in passionate flow, is the ecstasy of the conviction that *there* at least you are beloved; that there you are understood; that there your errors will meet ever with gentlest forgiveness; that there your troubles will be smiled away; that there you may unburden your soul, fearless of harsh, unsympathizing ears; and that there you may be entirely and joyfully — yourself.

There may be those of coarse mould — and I have seen such, even in the disguise of women — who will reckon these feelings puling sentiment. God pity them! as they have need of pity.

—— That image by the fireside, calm, loving, joyful, is there still; it goes not, however my spirit tosses, because my wish and every will keep it there unerring.

The fire shows through the screen, yellow and warm as a harvest sun. It is in its best age, and that age is ipeness.

A ripe heart! now I know what Wordsworth meant when he said, —

" The good die first,
And they whose hearts are dry as summer dust
Burn to the socket!"

The town-clock is striking midnight. The cold of the night wind is urging its way in at the door and window crevice; the fire has sunk almost to the third bar of the grate. Still my dream tires not, but wraps fondly round that image, now in the far-off, chilling mists of age, growing sainted. Love has blended into reverence; passion has subsided into joyous content.

—— And what if age comes? said I, in a new flush of excitation,— what else proves the wine? What else gives inner strength, and knowledge, and a steady pilot-hand, to steer your boat out boldly upon that shoreless sea where the river of life is running? Let the white ashes gather; let the silver hair lie where lay the auburn; let the eye gleam farther back, and dimmer; it is but retreating toward the pure sky-depths, an usher to the land where you will follow after.

It is quite cold, and I take away the screen altogether; there is a little glow yet, but presently the coal slips down below the third bar, with a rumbling sound, like that of coarse gravel falling into a new-dug grave.

—— She is gone!

Well, the heart has burned fairly, evenly, generously while there was mortality to kindle it; eternity wil surely kindle it better.

—— Tears indeed! but they are tears of thanksgiving, of resignation, and of hope.

And the eyes — full of those tears which ministering

angels bestow — climb with quick vision upon the an
gelic ladder, and open upon the futurity where she has
entered, and upon the country which she enjoys.

It is midnight, and the sounds of life are dead.

You are in the death-chamber of life; but you are also in the death-chamber of care. The world seem sliding backward; and hope and you are sliding forward. The clouds, the agonies, the vain expectancies the braggart noise, the fears, now vanish behind the curtain of the Past, and of the Night. They roll from your soul like a load.

In the dimness of what seems the ending Present, you reach out your prayerful hands toward that boundless Future, where God's eye lifts over the horizon like sunrise on the ocean. Do you recognize it as an earnest of something better? Aye, if the heart has been pure and steady,— burning like my fire,—it has learned it without seeming to learn. Faith has grown upon it as the blossom grows upon the bud, or the flower upon the slow-lifting stalk.

Cares cannot come into the dream-land where I live. They sink with the dying street noise, and vanish with the embers of my fire. Even Ambition, with its hot and shifting flame, is all gone out. The heart in the dimness of the fading fire-glow is all itself. The memory of what good things have come over it in the troubled youth life bear it up, and hope and faith bear it on

There is no extravagant pulse-glow; there is no mad fever of the brain; but only the soul, forgetting, for once, all, save its destinies and its capacities for good. And it mounts higher and higher on these wings of thought; and hope burns stronger and stronger out of the ashes of decaying life, until the sharp edge of the grave seems but a foot-scraper at the wicket of Elysium.

But what is paper; and what are words? Vain things! The soul leaves them behind; the pen staggers like a starveling cripple, and your heart is leaving it a whole length of the life-course behind. The soul's mortal longings, its poor baffled hopes, are dim now in the light of those infinite longings which spread over it, soft and holy as day-dawn. Eternity has stretched a corner of its mantle toward you, and the breath of its waving fringe is like a gale of Araby.

A little rumbling, and a last plunge of the cinders within my grate startled me, and dragged back my fancy from my flower chase, beyond the Phlegethon, to the white ashes that were now thick all over the darkened coals.

—— And this, mused I, is only a bachelor-dream about a pure and loving heart! And to-morrow comes cankerous life again: is it wished for? or, if not wished for, is the not wishing wicked?

Will dreams satisfy, reach high as they can? Are we not, after all, poor, grovelling mortals, tied to earth and to each other? Are there not sympathies, and hopes, and affections which can only find their issue and blessing in fellow absorption? Does not the heart, steady and pure as it may be, and mounting on soul-flights often as it dare, want a human sympathy perfectly indulged to make it healthful? Is there not a fount of love for this world, as there is a fount of love for the other? Is there not a certain store of tenderness cooped in this heart, which must and *will* be lavished before the end comes? Does it not plead with the judgment, and make issue with prudence, year after year? Does it not dog your steps all through your social pilgrimage, setting up its claims in forms fresh and odorous as new-blown heath-bells, saying, Come away from the heartless, the factitious, the vain, and measure your heart, not by its constraints, but by its fulness and by its depth? Let it run and be joyous!

Is there no demon that comes to your harsh night-dreams, like a taunting fiend, whispering, Be satisfied; keep your heart from running over; bridle those affections; there is nothing worth loving?

Does not some sweet being hover over your spirit of reverie like a beckoning angel, crowned with halo, saying, Hope on, hope ever; the heart and I are kindred our mission will be fulfilled; nature shall accomplish its purpose; the soul shall have its paradise?

—— I threw myself upon my bed; and as my

thoughts ran over the definite, sharp business of the morrow, my Reverie, and its glowing images that made my heart bound, swept away like those fleecy rain-clouds of August, on which the sun paints rainbows, driving southward, by a cool, rising wind from the north.

—— I wonder, thought I, as I dropped asleep, if a married man with his sentiment made actual, is, after all, as happy as we poor fellows in our dreams?

THIRD REVERIE.

A CIGAR THREE TIMES LIGHTED.

OVER HIS CIGAR.

I DO not believe that there was ever an Aunt Tabithy who could abide cigars. My Aunt Tabithy hated them with a peculiar hatred. She was not only insensible to the rich flavor of a fresh, rolling volume of smoke, but she could not so much as tolerate the sight of the rich russet color of a Havana-labelled box. It put her out of all conceit with Guava jelly, to find it advertised in the same tongue, and with the same Cuban coarseness of design.

She could see no good in a cigar.

"But by your leave, my aunt," said I to her, the other morning, "there is very much that is good in a cigar."

My aunt, who was sweeping, tossed her head, and with it her curls — done up in paper.

"It is a very excellent matter," continued I, puffing.

"It is dirty," said my aunt.

"It is clean and sweet," said I; "and a most pleasant soother of disturbed feelings; and a capital companion; and a comforter —" and I stopped to puff.

"You know it is a filthy abomination," said my aunt; "and you ought to be —" and she stopped to put up one of her curls, which, with the energy of her gesticulation, had fallen out of place.

"It suggests quiet thoughts," continued I; "and makes a man meditative; and gives a current to his habits of contemplation, — as I can show you," said I, warming with the theme.

My aunt, still fingering her papers, — with the pin in her mouth, — gave a most incredulous shrug.

"Aunt Tabithy," said I, and gave two or three violent, consecutive puffs, — "Aunt Tabithy, I can make up such a series of reflections out of my cigar, as would do your heart good to listen to!"

"About what, pray?" said my aunt, contemptuously.

"About love," said I, "which is easy enough lighted, but wants constancy to keep it in a glow. Or about matrimony, which has a great deal of fire in the beginning, but it is a fire that consumes all that feeds the blaze. Or about life," continued I, earnestly, "which at the first is fresh and odorous, but ends shortly in a withered cinder, that is fit only for the ground."

My aunt, who was forty and unmarried, finished her curl with a flip of the fingers, resumed her hold of the broom, and leaned her chin upon one end of it, with an expression of some wonder, some curiosity, and a great deal of expectation.

I could have wished my aunt had been a little less curious, or that I had been a little less communicative; for though it was all honestly said on my part, yet my contemplations bore that vague, shadowy, and delicious sweetness, that it seemed impossible to put them into words, — least of all, at the bidding of an old lady leaning on a broom-handle.

"Give me time, Aunt Tabithy," said I, "a good dinner, and after it a good cigar, and I will serve you such a sunshiny sheet of reverie, all twisted out of the smoke, as will make your kind old heart ache!"

Aunt Tabithy, in utter contempt, either of my mention of the dinner, or of the smoke, or of the old heart, commenced sweeping furiously.

"If I do not," continued I, anxious to appease her, — "if I do not, Aunt Tabithy, it shall be my last cigar; (Aunt Tabithy stopped sweeping;) and all my tobacco money (Aunt Tabithy drew near me) shall go to buy ribbons for my most respectable and worthy Aunt Tabithy; and a kinder person could not have them; or one," continued I, with a generous puff, "whom they would more adorn."

My Aunt Tabithy gave me a half-playful, half-thankful nudge.

It was in this way that our bargain was struck; my part of it is already stated. On her part, Aunt Tabithy was to allow me, in case of my success, an evening cigar unmolested, upon the front porch, underneath her favorite rose-tree. It was concluded, I say, as I sat; the smoke of my cigar rising gracefully around my Aunt Tabithy's curls; our right hands joined; my left was holding my cigar, while in hers was tightly grasped — her broomstick.

And this Reverie, to make the matter short, is what came of the contract.

L

Lighted with a Coal.

I TAKE up a coal with the tongs, and setting the end of my cigar against it, puff — and puff again but there is no smoke. There is very little hope of lighting from a dead coal; no more hope, thought I, than of kindling one's heart into flame by contact with a dead heart.

To kindle, there must be warmth and life; and I sat for a moment, thinking — even before I lit my cigar — on the vanity and folly of those poor, purblind fellows, who go on puffing for half a lifetime against dead coals. It is to be hoped that Heaven, in its mercy, has made their senses so obtuse, that they know not when their souls are in a flame, or when they are dead. I can imagine none but the most moderate satisfaction, in continuing to love what has got no ember of love within it. The Italians have a very sensible sort of proverb, — *amare, e non essere amato, è tempo perduto,* — to love, and not be loved, is time lost.

I take a kind of rude pleasure in flinging down a coal that has no life in it. And it seemed to me —

and may Heaven pardon the ill-nature that belongs to the thought — that there would be much of the same kind of satisfaction in dashing from you a luke warm creature, covered over with the yellow ashes of old combustion, that with ever so much attention, and the nearest approach of the lips, never shows signs of fire. May Heaven forgive me again, but I should long to break away, though the marriage bonds held me, and see what liveliness was to be found elsewhere.

I have seen before now a creeping vine try to grow up against a marble wall; it shoots out its tendrils in all directions, seeking for some crevice by which to fasten and to climb, — looking now above and now below, twining upon itself, reaching farther up, — but after all finding no good foothold, and falling away as if in despair. But nature is not unkind; twining things were made to twine. The longing tendrils take new strength in the sunshine and in the showers, and shoot out toward some hospitable trunk. They fasten easily to the kindly roughness of the bark, and stretch up, dragging after them the vine; which by-and-by, from the topmost bough, will nod its blossoms over at the marble wall that refused it succor, as if it said, — Stand there in your pride, cold, white wall! we, the tree and I, are kindred; it the helper, and I the helped; and, bound fast together, we riot in the sunshine and in gladness.

The thought of this image made me search for a new coal that should have some brightness in it. There may be a white ash over it, indeed, — as you will find tender feelings covered with the mask of courtesy, or with the veil of fear, — but with a breath it all flies off, and exposes the heat and the glow that you are seeking

At the first touch, the delicate edges of the cigar crimple, a thin line of smoke rises, — doubtfully for a while, and with a coy delay; but after a hearty respiration or two, it grows strong, and my cigar is fairly lighted.

That first taste of the new smoke and of the fragrant leaf is very grateful; it has a bloom about it that you wish might last. It is like your first love, — fresh, genial, and rapturous. Like that, it fills up all the craving of your soul; and the light, blue wreaths of smoke, like the roseate clouds that hang around the morning of your heart-life, cut you off from the chill atmosphere of mere worldly companionship, and make a gorgeous firmament for your fancy to riot in.

I do not speak now of those later and manlier passions, into which judgment must be thrusting its cold tones, and when all the sweet tumult of your heart has mellowed into the sober ripeness of affection. But I mean that boyish burning which belongs to every poor mortal's lifetime, and which bewilders him with the thought that he has reached the highest point of human joy, before he has tasted any of that bitterness from which alone our highest human joys have spring. I mean the time when you cut initials with your jack-knife on the smooth bark of beech-trees; and went moping under the long shadows at sunset; and thought Louise the prettiest name in the wide world; and picked flowers to leave at her door; and stole out at night to watch the light in her window; and read such novels as those about Helen Mar, or Charlotte, to give some adequate expression to your agonized feelings.

At such a stage, you are quite certain that you are deeply and madly in love; you persist, in the face of heaven and earth. You would like to meet the individual who dared to doubt it.

You think she has got the tidiest and jauntiest little figure that ever was seen. You think back upon some time when, in your games of forfeit, you gained a kiss from those lips; and it seems as if the kiss was hanging on you yet, and warming you all over. And then again, it seems so strange that your lips did really touch hers! You half question if it could have been actually so,—and how you could have dared; and you wonder if you would have courage to do the same thing again? and upon second thought are quite sure you would, and snap your fingers at the thought of it.

What sweet little hats she does wear; and in the school-room, when the hat is hung up, what curls!

golden curls, worth a hundred Golcondas! How bravely you study the top lines of the spelling-book, that your eyes may run over the edge of the cover without the schoolmaster's notice, and feast upon her!

You half wish that somebody would run away with her, as they did with Amanda, in the "Children of the Abbey"; and then you might ride up on a splendid black horse, and draw a pistol or blunderbuss, and shoot the villains, and carry her back, all in tears, fainting and languishing upon your shoulder, and have her father (who is Judge of the County Court) take your hand in both of his, and make some eloquent remarks. A great many such recaptures you run over in your mind, and think how delightful it would be to peril your life, either by flood or fire, — to cut off your arm, or your head, or any such trifle, for your dear Louise.

You can hardly think of anything more joyous in life than to live with her in some old castle, very far away from steamboats and post-offices, and pick wild geraniums for her hair, and read poetry with her under the shade of very dark ivy vines. And you would have such a charming boudoir in some corner of the old ruin, with a harp in it, and books bound in gilt, with cupids on the cover, and such a fairy couch, with the curtains hung — as you have seen them hung in some illustrated Arabian stories — upon a pair of carved doves!

And when they laugh at you about it, you turn it off

perhaps, with saying, "It is n't so;" but afterward, in your chamber, or under the tree where you have cut her name, you take Heaven to witness that it is so, and think, What a cold world it is, to be so careless about such holy emotions! You perfectly hate a certain stout boy in a green jacket, who is forever twitting you, and calling her names; but when some old maiden aunt teases you in her kind, gentle way, you bear it very proudly, and with a feeling as if you could bear a great deal more for *her* sake. And when the minister reads off marriage announcements in the church, you think how it will sound, one of these days, to have your name and hers read from the pulpit; and how the people will all look at you, and how prettily she will blush; and how poor little Dick — who you know loves her, but is afraid to say so — will squirm upon his bench.

—— Heigho! mused I, — as the blue smoke rolled up around my head, — these first kindlings of the love that is in one are very pleasant! but will they last?

You love to listen to the rustle of her dress, as she stirs about the room. It is better music than grown-up ladies will make upon all their harpsichords, in the years that are to come. But this, thank Heaven, you do not know.

You think you can trace her footmark, on your way to the school; and what a dear little footmark it is! And from that single point, if she be out of your sight for days, you conjure up the whole image: the elastic, lithe little figure, — the springy step, — the dotted muslin, so light and flowing, — the silk kerchief, with its most tempting fringe playing upon the clear white of her throat; how you envy that fringe! And her chin is as round as a peach; and the lips, — such lips! and you sigh, and hang your head, and wonder when you *shall* see her again!

You would like to write her a letter; but then, people would talk so coldly about it; and, beside, you are not quite sure you could write such billets as Thaddeus of Warsaw used to write, and anything less warm or elegant would not do at all. You talk about this one or that one, whom they call pretty, in the coolest way in the world: you see very little of their prettiness; they are good girls, to be sure; and you hope they will get good husbands some day or other; but it is not a matter that concerns you very much. They do not live in your world of romance; they are not the angels of that sky which your heart makes rosy, and to which I have likened the blue waves of this rolling smoke.

You can even joke as you talk of others; you can smile — as you think — very graciously; you can say laughingly that you are deeply in love with them, and think it a most capital joke; you can touch their hands, or steal a kiss from them in your games, most imperturbably; — they are very dead coals.

But the live one is very lively. When you take the name on your lip, it seems, somehow, to be made of different materials from the rest; you cannot half so easily separate it into letters; write it, indeed, you can, for you have had practice, very much private practice on odd scraps of paper, and on the fly-leaves of geographies, and of your natural philosophy. You know perfectly well how it looks; it seems to be written, indeed somewhere behind your eyes, and in such happy position, with respect to the optic nerve, that you see it all the time, though you are looking in an opposite direction, — and so distinctly, that you have great fears lest people looking into your eyes should see it too.

For all this, it is a far more delicate name to handle than most that you know of. Though it is very cool and pleasant on the brain, it is very hot and difficult to manage on the lip. It is not, as your schoolmaster would say, a name, so much as it is an idea; not a noun, but a verb, — an active, and transitive verb; and yet a most irregular verb, wanting the passive voice.

It is something against your schoolmaster's doctrine, to find warmth in the moonlight; but with that soft hand — it is very soft — lying within your arm, there is a great deal of warmth, whatever the philosophers may say, even in pale moonlight. The beams, too, breed sympathies, very close-running sympathies, not talked about in the chapters on optics, and altogether too fine for language. And, under their influence, you retain the little hand that you had not dared retain so long before; and her struggle to recover it — if indeed it be a struggle — is infinitely less than it was; nay it is a kind of struggle, not so much against you, as between gladness and modesty. It makes you as bold as a lion; and the feeble hand, like a poor lamb in the lion's clutch, is powerless, and very meek; and failing of escape, it will sue for gentle treatment, and will meet your warm promise with a kind of grateful pressure, that is but half acknowledged by the hand that makes it.

My cigar is burning with wondrous freeness; and from the smoke flash forth images bright and quick as lightning, with no thunder but the thunder of the pulse. But will it all last? Damp will deaden the fire of a cigar; and there are hellish damps — alas! too many— that will deaden the early blazing of the heart.

She is pretty, — growing prettier to your eye the more you look upon her, and prettier to your ear the more you listen to her. But you wonder who the tall boy was, whom you saw walking with her two days ago. He was not a bad-looking boy; on the contrary, you think (with a grit of your teeth) that he was infernally handsome. You look at him very shyly and very closely when you pass him, and turn to see how he walks, and to measure his shoulders, and are quite disgusted with the very modest and gentlemanly way with which he carries himself. You think you would like to have a fisticuff with him, if you were only sure of having the best of it. You sound the neighborhood coyly, to find out who the strange boy is, and are half ashamed of yourself for doing it.

You gather a magnificent bouquet to send her, and tie it with a green ribbon and love-knot; and get a little rose-bud in acknowledgment. *That* day you pass the tall boy with a very patronizing look, and wonder if he would not like to have a sail in *your* boat?

But by-and-by you find the tall boy walking with her again; and she looks sideways at him, and with a kind of grown-up air that makes you feel very boylike, and humble, and furious. And you look daggers at him when you pass, and touch your cap to her with quite uncommon dignity,— and wonder if she is not sorry, and does not feel very badly, to have got such a look from you?

On some other day, however, you meet her alone; and the sight of her makes your face wear a genial, sunny air; and you talk a little sadly about your fears and your jealousies. She seems a little sad and a little glad, together, and is sorry she has made you feel badly,— and you are sorry too. And with this pleasant twin sorrow you are knit together again — closer than ever. That one little tear of hers has been worth more to you than a thousand smiles. Now you love her madly; you could swear it, — swear it to her, or swear it to the universe. You even say as much to some kind old friend at nightfall; but your mention of her is tremulous and joyful, with a kind of bound in your speech, as if the heart worked too quick for the tongue, and as if the lips were ashamed to be passing over such secrets of the soul to the mere sense of hearing. At this stage you cannot trust yourself to speak her praises; or if you venture, the expletives fly away with your thought before you can chain it into language; and your speech, at your best endeavor, is but a succession of broken superlatives that you are ashamed of. You strain for language that will scald the thought of her; but hot as you can make it, it falls back upon your heated fancy like a cold shower.

Heat so intense as this consumes very fast; and the matter it feeds fastest on is — judgment; and with judgment gone, there is room for jealousy to creep in. You grow petulant at another sight of that tall boy; and the one tear, which cured your first petulance, will not cure it now. You let a little of your fever break out in speech — a speech which you go home to mourn over. But she knows nothing of the mourning, while she knows very much of the anger. Vain tears are very apt to breed pride; and when you go again with your petulance, you will find your rosy-lipped girl taking her first studies in dignity.

You will stay away, you say: poor fool, you are feeding on what your disease loves best! You wonder if she is not sighing for your return, and if your name is not running in her thought, and if tears of regret are not moistening those sweet eyes.

—— And wondering thus, you stroll moodily and hopefully toward her father's home; you pass the door once, twice; you loiter under the shade of an old tree where you have sometimes bid her adieu; your old fondness is struggling with your pride, and has almost made the mastery; but in the very moment of victory you see yonder your hated rival, and beside him, looking very gleeful and happy,— your perfidious Louise.

How quick you throw off the marks of your struggle, and put on the boldest air of boyhood; and what a dexterous handling to your knife, and a wonderful keenness to the edge, as you cut away from the bark of the beech-tree all trace of her name! Still, there is a little silent relenting, and a few tears at night, and a little tremor of the hand, as you tear out, the next day, every fly-leaf that bears her name. But at sight of your rival — looking so jaunty, and in such capital spirits — you put on the proud man again. You may meet her, but you say nothing of your struggles; oh, no! not one word of that; but you talk with amazing rapidity about your games, or what not; and you never — never give her another peep into your boyish heart.

For a week, you do not see her,— nor for a month,— nor two months, — nor three.

——— Puff, puff, once more. There is only a little nauseous smoke; and now — my cigar is gone out altogether. I must light again.

With a Wisp of Paper.

THERE are those who throw away a cigar when once gone out; they must needs have plenty more. But nobody that I ever heard of keeps a cedar box of hearts labelled at Havana. Alas! there is but one to light!

But can a heart once lit be lighted again? Authority on this point is worth something; yet it should be impartial authority. I should be loth to take in evidence for the fact — however it should tally with my hope — the affidavit of some rakish old widower, who had cast his weeds before the grass had started on the mound of his affliction; and I should be as slow to take, in way of rebutting testimony, the oath of any sweet young girl just becoming conscious of her heart's existence — by its loss.

Very much, it seems to me, depends upon the quality of the fire; and I can easily conceive of one so pure, so constant, so exhausting, that, if it were once gone out, whether in the chills of death, or under the blasts of pitiless fortune, there would be no rekindling, simply because there would be nothing left to kindle. And I can imagine, too, a fire so earnest and so true, that, whatever malice might urge, or a devilish ingenuity devise, there could no other be found, high or low, far or near, which should not so contrast with the first as to make it seem cold as ice.

I remember, in an old play of Davenport's, the hero is led to doubt his mistress; he is worked upon by slanders to quit her altogether, though he has loved, and does still love passionately. She bids him adieu, with large tears dropping from her eyes; (and I lay down my cigar, to recite it aloud, fancying all the while, with a varlet impudence, that some Abstemia is repeating it to me :)

—— "Farewell, Lorenzo,
Whom my soul doth love; if you ever marry,
May you meet a good wife; so good, that you
May not suspect her, nor may she be worthy
Of your suspicion: and if you hear hereafter
That I am dead, inquire but my last words,
And you shall know that to the last I loved you.
And when you walk forth with your second choice
Into the pleasant fields, and by chance talk of me,
Imagine that you see me lean and pale,
Strewing your paths with flowers!" *

—— Poor Abstemia! Lorenzo never could find such another; there never could be such another, for such Lorenzo.

* *The City Night-Cap*, Act ii. Sc. 2.

To blaze anew, it is essential that the old fire be utterly gone; and can any truly-lighted soul ever grow cold, except the grave cover it? The poets all say no Othello, had he lived a thousand years, would not have loved again; nor Desdemona, — nor Andromache, — nor Medea, — nor Ulysses, — nor Hamlet. But in the cool wreaths of the pleasant smoke, let us see what truth is in the poets.

—— What is love, mused I, at the first, but a mere fancy? There is a prettiness that your soul cleaves to, as your eye to a pleasant flower, or your ear to a soft melody. Presently, admiration comes in, as a sort of balance-wheel for the eccentric revolutions of your fancy, and your admiration is touched off with such neat quality as respect. Too much of this, indeed, they say, deadens the fancy, and so retards the action of the heart-machinery. But with a proper modicum to serve as a stock, devotion is grafted in; and then, by an agreeable and confused mingling, all these qualities and affections of the soul become transfused into that vital feeling called Love.

Your heart seems to have gone over to another and better counterpart of your humanity; what is left of you seems the mere husk of some kernel that has been stolen. It is not an emotion of yours, which is making very easy voyages towards another soul, — that may be shortened or lengthened at will; but it is a passion that is only yours because it is *there;* the more it lodges there, the more keenly you feel it to be yours.

The qualities that feed this passion may, indeed, belong to you, but they never gave birth to such an one before, simply because there was no place in which it could grow. Nature is very provident in these matters. The chrysalis does not burst until there is a wing to help the gauze-fly upward. The shell does not break until the bird can breathe; nor does the swallow quit its nest until its wings are tipped with the airy oars.

This passion of love is strong, just in proportion as the atmosphere it finds is tender of its life. Let that atmosphere change into too great coldness, and the passion becomes a wreck, — not yours, because it is not worth your having, — nor vital, because it has lost the soil where it grew. But is it not laying the reproach in a high quarter, to say that those qualities of the heart, which begot this passion, are exhausted, and will not thenceforth germinate through all of your lifetime?

——Take away the worm-eaten frame from your arbor plant, and the wrenched arms of the despoiled climber will not, at the first, touch any new trellis; they cannot in a day change the habit of a year. But let the new support stand firmly, and the needy tendrils will presently lay hold upon the stranger; and your plant will regain its pride and pomp, — cherishing, perhaps, in its bent figure, a memento of the Old, but in its more earnest and abounding life mindful only of its sweet dependence on the New.

Let the poets say what they will, these affections of ours are not blind, stupid creatures, to starve under polar snows, when the very breezes of Heaven are the appointed messengers to guide them toward warmth and sunshine!

―― And with a little suddenness of manner I tear off a wisp of paper, and holding it in the blaze of my lamp, relight my cigar. It does not burn so easily, perhaps, as at first; it wants warming before it will catch; but presently it is in a broad, full glow, that throws light into the corners of my room.

―― Just so, thought I, the love of youth, which succeeds the crackling blaze of boyhood, makes a broader flame, though it may not be so easily kindled. A mere dainty step, or a curling lock, or a soft blue eye, are not enough; but in her who has quickened the new blaze there is a blending of all these, with a certain sweetness of soul that finds expression in whatever feature or motion you look upon. Her charms steal over you gently, and almost imperceptibly. You think that she is a pleasant companion, ― nothing more; and you find the opinion strongly confirmed day by day, ― so wel confirmed, indeed, that you begin to wonder why it is that she is such a delightful companion? It cannot be her eye, for you have seen eyes almost as pretty as

Nelly's; nor can it be her mouth, though Nelly's mouth is certainly very sweet. And you keep studying what on earth it can be that makes you so earnest to be near her, or to listen to her voice. The study is pleasant you do not know any study that is more so, or which you accomplish with less mental fatigue.

Upon a sudden, some fine day, when the air is balmy and the recollection of Nelly's voice and manner more balmy still, you wonder if you are in love? When a man has such a wonder, he is either very near love, or he is very far away from it; it is a wonder that is either suggested by his hope, or by that entanglement of feeling which blunts all his perceptions.

But if not in love, you have at least a strong fancy; so strong, that you tell your friends carelessly that she is a nice girl, nay, a beautiful girl; and if your education has been bad, you strengthen the epithet on your own tongue with a very wicked expletive, of which the mildest form would be — "deuced fine girl!" Presently, however, you get beyond this, and your companionship and your wonder relapse into a constant, quiet habit of unmistakable love, — not impulsive, quick, and fiery, like the first, but mature and calm. It is as if it were born with your soul; and the recognition of t was rather an old remembrance than a fresh passion. It does not seek to gratify its exuberance and force with such relief as night-serenades, or any Jacques-like med itations in the forest; but it is a quiet, still joy, that floats on your hope into the years to come, making the prospect all sunny and joyful.

It is a kind of oil and balm for whatever was stormy or harmful; it gives a permanence to the smile of existence. It does not make the sea of your life turbulent with high emotions, as if a strong wind were blowing, but it is as if an Aphrodite had broken on the surface, and the ripples were spreading with a sweet, low sound, and widening far out to the very shores of Time.

There is no need now, as with the boy, to bolster up your feelings with extravagant vows; even should you try this in her presence, the words are lacking to put such vows in. So soon as you reach them, they fail you; and the oath only quivers on the lip, or tells its story by a pressure of the fingers. You wear a brusque, pleasant air with your acquaintances, and hint — with a sly look — at possible changes in your circumstances. Of an evening, you are kind to the most unattractive of the wall-flowers, — if only your Nelly is away; and you have a sudden charity for street-beggars with pale children. You catch yourself taking a step in one of the new polkas, upon a country walk; and wonder immensely at the number of bright days which succeed each other, without leaving a single stormy gap for your old melancholy moods. Even the chambermaids at your hotel never did their duty one half so well; and as for your man Tom, he is become a perfect pattern of a fellow.

My cigar is in a fine glow; but it has gone out once, and it may go out again.

—— You begin to talk of marriage; but some obstinate papa or guardian uncle thinks that it will never do, — that it is quite too soon, or that Nelly is a mere girl. Or some of your wild oats — quite forgotten by yourself — shoot up on the vision of a staid mamma, and throw a very damp shadow on your character. Or the old lady has an ambition of another sort, which you, a simple, earnest, plodding bachelor, can never gratify; — being of only passable appearance, and unschooled in the fashions of the world, you will be eternally rubbing the elbows of the old lady's pride.

All this will be strangely afflictive to one who has been living for quite a number of weeks or months in a pleasant dream-land, where there were no five per cents, or reputations, but only a very full and delirious flow of feeling. What care you for any position, except a position near the being that you love? What wealth do you prize, except a wealth of heart that shall never know diminution; or for reputation, except that of truth and of honor? How hard it would break upon these pleasant idealities to have a weazen-faced old guardian set his arm in yours, and tell you how tenderly he has at heart the happiness of his niece; and reason with you about your very small and sparse dividends, **and** your limited business; and caution you — for he has **a** lively regard for your interests — about continuing your addresses?

―――― The kind old curmudgeon!

Your man Tom has grown suddenly a very stupid fellow; and all your charity for withered wall-flowers is gone. Perhaps, in your wrath, the suspicion comes over you that she too wishes you were something higher, or more famous, or richer, or anything but what you are! — a very dangerous suspicion; for no man with any true nobility of soul can ever make his heart the slave of another's condescension.

But no! you will not, you cannot believe this of Nelly. That face of hers is too mild and gracious; and her manner, as she takes your hand after your heart is made sad, and turns away those rich blue eyes, shadowed more deeply than ever by the long and moistened fringe, — and the exquisite softness and meaning of the pressure of those little fingers, — and the low, half sob, — and the heaving of that bosom in its struggles between love and duty, — all forbid. Nelly, you could swear, is tenderly indulgent — like the fond creature that she is — toward all your shortcomings, and would not barter your strong love and your honest heart for the greatest magnate in the land.

What a spur to effort is the confiding love of a **true**-

hearted woman! That last fond look of hers, hopeful and encouraging, has more power within it to nerve your soul to high deeds than all the admonitions of all your tutors. Your heart, beating large with hope, quickens the flow upon the brain, and you make wild vows to win greatness. But alas! this is a great world — very full and very rough, —

> "all up-hill work when we would do;
> All down-hill, when we suffer." *

Hard, withering toil only can achieve a name; and long days and months and years must be passed in the chase of that bubble — reputation; which, when once grasped, breaks in your eager clutch into a hundred lesser bubbles that soar above you still.

A clandestine meeting from time to time, and a note or two tenderly written, keep up the blaze in your heart. But presently the lynx-eyed old guardian — so tender of your interests and hers — forbids even this irregular and unsatisfying correspondence. Now you can feed yourself only on stray glimpses of her figure, as full of sprightliness and grace as ever; and that beaming face, you are half sorry to see from time to time, still beautiful. You struggle with your moods of melancholy and wear bright looks yourself, — bright to her, and very bright to the eye of the old curmudgeon who has

* *Festus.*

snatched your heart away. It will never do to show your weakness to a man.

At length, on some pleasant morning, you learn that she is gone, — too far away to be seen, too closely guarded to be reached. For a while you throw down your books, and abandon your toil in despair, thinking very bitter thoughts, and making very hopeless resolves.

My cigar is still burning; but it will require constan and strong respiration to keep it in a glow.

A letter or two, dispatched at random, relieve the excess of your fever, until, with practice, these random letters have even less heat in them than the heat of your study or of your business. Grief, thank God! is not so progressive or so cumulative as joy. For a time there is a pleasure in the mood with which you recall your broken hopes, and with which you selfishly link hers to the shattered wreck; but absence and ignorance tame the point of your woe. You call up the image of Nelly adorning other and distant scenes. You see the tearful smile give place to a blithesome cheer; and the thought of you, that shaded her fair face so long, fades under the sunshine of gayety; or, at best, it only seems to cross that white forehead like a playful shadow that a fleecy cloud-remnant will fling upon a sunny lawn.

As for you, the world, with its whirl and roar, is deafening the sweet, distant notes that come up through old, choked channels of the affections. Life is calling for earnestness, and not for regrets. So the months and the years slip by; your bachelor habit grows easy and light with wearing; you have mourned enough to smile at the violent mourning of others; and you have enjoyed enough to sigh over their little eddies of delight. Dark shades and delicious streaks of crimson and gold color lie upon your life. Your heart, with all its weight of ashes, can yet sparkle at the sound of a fairy step, and your face can yet open into a round of joyous smiles — that are almost hopes — in the presence of some bright-eyed girl.

But amid this there will float over you, from time to time, a midnight trance, in which you will hear again with a thirsty ear the witching melody of the days that are gone; and you will wake from it with a shudder into the cold resolves of your lonely and manly life. But the shudder passes as easy as night from morning. Tearful regrets, and memories that touch to the quick, are dull weapons to break through the panoply of your seared, eager, and ambitious manhood. They only venture out, like timid, white-winged flies, when night is come; and at the first glimpse of the dawn they shrivel up, and lie without a flutter in some corner of your soul.

And when, years after, you learn that she has returned — a woman, there is a slight glow, but no tumultuous bound of the heart. Life and time have worried you down like a spent hound. The world has given you a habit of easy and unmeaning smiles. You half accuse yourself of ingratitude and forgetfulness; but the accusation does not oppress you. It does not even distract your attention from the morning journal. You cannot work yourself into a respectable degree of indignation against the old gentleman — her guardian.

You sigh — poor thing! — and in a very flashy waist coat you venture a morning call.

She meets you kindly, — a comely, matronly dame in gingham, with her curls all gathered under a high-topped comb; and she presents to you two little boys in smart crimson jackets dressed up with braid. And you dine with Madame — a family party; and the weazen-faced old gentleman meets you with a most pleasant shake of the hand, — hints that you were among his niece's earliest friends, and hopes that you are getting on well.

—— Capitally well!

And the boys toddle in at dessert, — Dick, to get a plum from your own dish; Tom, to be kissed by his rosy-faced papa. In short, you are made perfectly at home; and you sit over your wine for an hour, in a cosy smoke with the gentlemanly uncle, and with the very courteous husband of your second flame.

It is all very jovial at the table; for good wine is, I find, a great strengthener of the bachelor heart. But afterward, when night has fairly set in, and the blaze of your fire goes flickering over your lonely quarters, you heave a deep sigh. And as your thought runs back to the perfidious Louise, and calls up the married and matronly Nelly, you sob over that poor dumb heart within you, which craves so madly a free and joyous utterance! And as you lean over, with your forehead in your hands, and your eyes fall upon the old hound slumbering on the rug, the tears start, and you wish that you had married years ago, and that you too had your pair of prattling boys, to drive away the loneliness of your solitary hearth-stone.

—— My cigar would not go ; it was fairly out. But, with true bachelor obstinacy, I vowed that I would light again.

III.

Lighted with a Match.

I HATE a match. I feel sure that brimstone matches were never made in heaven; and it is sad to think that, with few exceptions, matches are all of them tipped with brimstone.

But my taper having burned out, and the coals being all dead upon the hearth, a match is all that is left to me.

All matches will not blaze on the first trial; and there are those that, with the most indefatigable coaxings, never show a spark. They may indeed leave in their trail phosphorescent streaks, but you can no more light your cigar at them than you can kindle your heart at the covered wife-trails which the infernal, gossiping, old match-makers will lay in your path.

Was there ever a bachelor of seven-and-twenty, I wonder, who has not been haunted by pleasant old ladies, and trim, excellent, good-natured married friends, who talk to him about nice matches — "very nice matches," — matches which never go off? And who, pray, has not had some kind old uncle to fill two sheets for him (perhaps in the time of heavy postages) about some most eligible connection — " of highly respectable parentage!"

What a delightful thing, surely, for a withered bachelor, to bloom forth in the dignity of an ancestral tree What a precious surprise for him, who has all his life worshipped the wing-heeled Mercury, to find on a sudden a great stock of preserved and most respectable Penates!

—— In God's name, thought I, puffing vehemently, what is a man's heart given him for, if not to choose where his heart's blood, every drop of it, is flowing? Who is going to dam these billowy tides of the soul, whose roll is ordered by a planet greater than the moon, and that planet — Venus? Who is going to shift this vane of my desires, when every breeze that passes in my heaven is keeping it all the more strongly to its fixed bearings?

Besides this, there are the money-matches, urged upon you by disinterested bachelor friends, who would be very proud to see you at the head of an establishment. And I must confess that this kind of talk has a pleasant jingle about it, and is one of the cleverest aids to a bachelor's day-dreams that can well be imagined. And let not the pouting lady condemn me without a hearing.

It is certainly cheerful to think — for a contemplative bachelor — that the pretty ermine which so sets off the transparent hue of your imaginary wife, or the lace which lies so bewitchingly upon the superb roundness of her form, or the graceful bodice, trimmed to a line, which is of such exquisite adaptation to her lithe figure, will be always at her command; nay, that these are only units among the chameleon hues, under which you shall feed upon her beauty! I want to know if it is not a pretty cabinet picture for fancy to luxuriate upon — that of a sweet wife, who is cheating hosts of friends into love, sympathy, and admiration, by the modest munificence of her wealth? Is it not rather agreeable to feed your hopeful soul upon that abundance, which, while it supplies her need, will give a range to her loving charities; which will keep from her brow the shadows of anxiety, and will sublime her gentle nature, by adding to it the grace of an angel of mercy?

Is it not rich, in those days when the pestilent humors of bachelorhood hang heavy on you, to foresee in that shadowy realm, where hope is a native, the quiet of a home made splendid with attractions, and made real by the presence of her who bestows them? Upon my word, — thought I, as I continued puffing, — such a match must make a very grateful lighting of one's inner sympathies; nor am I prepared to say that such associations would not add force to the most abstract love imaginable.

Think of it for a moment: what is it that we poor fellows love? We love — if one may judge for himself, over his cigar — gentleness, beauty, refinement, generosity, and intelligence, — and far above these, a returning love, made up of all these qualities, and gaining upon your love, day by day and month by month, like a sunny morning gaining upon the frosts of night.

But wealth is a great means of refinement; and it is a security for gentleness, since it removes disturbing anxieties; and it is a pretty promoter of intelligence, since it multiplies the avenues for its reception; and it is a good basis for a generous habit of life: it even equips beauty, neither hardening its hand with toil, nor tempting the wrinkles to come early. But whether it provokes greatly that returning passion, that abnegation of soul, that sweet trustfulness and abiding affection which are to clothe your heart with joy, is far more doubtful. Wealth, while it gives so much, asks much in return; and the soul that is grateful to mammon is not over-ready to be grateful for intensity of love. It is hard to gratify those who have nothing left to gratify.

Heaven help the man, who, having wearied his soul with delays and doubts, or exhausted the freshness and exuberance of his youth by a hundred little dallyings of love, consigns himself at length to the issues of what people call a nice match, — whether of money, or of a family!

Heaven help you (I brushed the ashes from my cigar) when you begin to regard marriage as only a respectable institution, and under the advices of staid old friends begin to look about you for some very respectable wife. You may admire her figure, and her family, and bear pleasantly in mind the very casual mention which has been made by some of your penetrating friends that she has large expectations. You think that she would make a very capital appearance at the head of your table; nor, in the event of your coming to any public honor, would she make you blush for her breeding. She talks well, exceedingly well; and her face has its charms, especially under a little excitement. Her dress is elegant and tasteful, and she is constantly remarked upon by all your friends as a "nice person." Some good old lady, in whose pew she occasionally sits on a Sunday, or to whom she has sometimes sent a *papier-maché* card-case for the show-box of some Dorcas benevolent society, thinks, with a sly wink, that she would make a fine wife for — somebody.

She certainly *has* an elegant figure, and the marriage of some half-dozen of your old flames warn you that time is slipping and your chances failing. And in the pleasant warmth of some after-dinner mood you resolve — with her image in her prettiest pelisse drifting across your brain — that you will marry. Now comes the pleasant excitement of the chase; and whatever family dignity may surround her, only adds to the pleasurable glow of the pursuit. You give an hour more to your toilette, and a hundred or two more a year to your tailor. All is orderly, dignified, and gracious. Charlotte is a sensible woman, everybody says; and you believe it yourself. You agree in your talk about books, and churches, and flowers. Of course she has good taste — for she accepts you. The acceptance is dignified, elegant, and even courteous.

You receive numerous congratulations; and your old friend Tom writes you — that he hears you are going to marry a splendid woman; and all the old ladies say — what a capital match! And your business partner, who is a married man and something of a wag, " sympathizes sincerely." Upon the whole, you feel a little proud of your arrangement. You write to an old friend in the country that you are to marry presently Miss Charlotte of such a street, whose father was something very fine in his way, and whose father before him was very distinguished; you add, in a postscript, that she is easily situated, and has " expectations." Your friend, who has a wife that he loves and that loves him, writes back kindly, — " hoping you may be happy; " and hoping so yourself, you light your cigar — one of your last bachelor cigars — with the margin of his letter.

The match goes off with a brilliant marriage, — at which you receive a very elegant welcome from your wife's spinster cousins, and drink a great deal of champagne with her bachelor uncles. And as you take the dainty hand of your bride, — very magnificent under that bridal wreath, and with her face lit up by a brilliant glow, — your eye and your soul for the first time grow full. And as your arm circles that elegant figure, and you draw her toward you, feeling that she is yours, there is a bound at your heart that makes you think your soul-life is now whole and earnest. All your early dreams and imaginations come flowing on your thought like bewildering music; and as you gaze upon her, — the admiration of that crowd, — it seems to you that all that your heart prizes is made good by the accident of marriage.

— Ah, thought I, brushing off the ashes again, bridal pictures are not home pictures, and the hour at the altar is but a poor type of the waste of years!

Your household is elegantly ordered; Charlotte has secured the best of housekeepers, and she meets the compliments of your old friends, who come to dine with you, with a suavity that is never at fault. And they tell you — after the cloth is removed, and you sit quietly smoking in memory of the olden times — that she is a splendid woman. Even the old ladies who come for occasional charities, think Madame a pattern of a lady; and so think her old admirers, whom she receives still with an easy grace that half puzzles you. And as you stand by the ballroom door, at two of the morning, with your Charlotte's shawl upon your arm, some little panting fellow will confirm the general opinion by telling you that Madame is a magnificent dancer; and Monsieur le Comte will praise extravagantly her French. You are grateful for all this; but you have an uncommonly serious way of expressing your gratitude.

You think you ought to be a very happy fellow; and yet long shadows do steal over your thought, and you wonder that the sight of your Charlotte in the dress you used to admire so much does not scatter them to the winds; but it does not. You feel coy about putting your arm around that delicately robed figure, — you might derange the plaitings of her dress. She is civil towards you, and tender towards your bachelor friends. She talks with dignity, — adjusts her lace cape, — and hopes you will make a figure in the world, for the sake of the family. Her cheek is never soiled with a tear and her smiles are frequent, especially when you have some spruce young fellows at your table.

You catch sight of occasional notes perhaps, whose superscription you do not know; and some of her admirers' attentions become so pointed and constant that your pride is stirred. It would be silly to show jealousy; but you suggest to your "dear"—as you sip your tea—the slight impropriety of her action.

Perhaps you fondly long for some little scene, as a proof of wounded confidence; but no—nothing of that; she trusts (calling you "my dear") that she knows how to sustain the dignity of her position.

You are too sick at heart for comment, or for reply.

—— And is this the intertwining of soul, of which you had dreamed in the days that are gone? Is this the blending of sympathies that was to steal from life its bitterness, and spread over care and suffering the sweet ministering hand of kindness and of love? Aye, you may well wander back to your bachelor club, and make the hours long at the journals, or at play,—killing the flagging lapse of your life! Talk sprightly with your old friends, and mimic the joy you have not,—or you will wear a bad name upon your hearth, and head. Never suffer your Charlotte to catch sight of the tears which in bitter hours may start from your eye; or to hear the sighs which in your times of solitary musings may break forth sudden and heavy. Go on counterfeiting your life as you have begun. It was a nice match; and you are a nice husband!

But you have a little boy, thank God! toward whom your heart runs out freely; and you love to catch him 'n his respite from your well-ordered nursery and the tasks of his teachers—alone; and to spend upon him a little of that depth of feeling which through so many years has scarce been stirred. You play with him at his games; you fondle him; you take him to your bosom.

— But papa, he says, see how you have tumbled my collar. What shall I tell mamma?

—— Tell her, my boy, that I love you!

Ah! thought I, (my cigar was getting dull and nauseous,) is there not a spot in your heart that the gloved hand of your elegant wife has never reached, — that you wish it might reach?

You go to see a far-away friend: his was not a "nice match"; he was married years before you, and yet the beaming looks of his wife, and his lively smile, are as fresh and honest as they were years ago; and they make you ashamed of your disconsolate humor. Your stay is lengthened, but the home letters are not urgent for your return; yet they are marvellously proper letters, and rounded with a French *adieu*. You could have wished a little scrawl from your boy at the bottom, in the place of the postscript which gives you the names of a new opera troupe, and you hint as much, — a very bold stroke for you.

Ben, she says, writes too shamefully.

And at your return there is no great anticipation of delight; in contrast with the old dreams that a pleasant summer's journey has called up, your parlor, as you enter it, — so elegant, so still, so modish, — seems the charnel-house of your heart.

By-and-by you fall into weary days of sickness; you have capital nurses, nurses highly recommended, nurses who never make mistakes, nurses who have served long in the family. But alas for that heart of sympathy, and for that sweet face shaded with your pain, — like a soft landscape with flying clouds, — you have none of them. Your pattern wife may come in, from time to time, to look after your nurse, or to ask after your sleep, and glide out, — her silk dress rustling upon the door, like dead leaves in the cool night-breezes of winter. Or perhaps, after putting this chair in its place, and adjusting to a more tasteful fold that curtain, she will ask you, with a tone that might mean sympathy if it were not a stranger to you, if she can do anything more.

Thank her, as kindly as you can, and close your eyes, and dream; or rouse up, to lay your hand upon the head of your little boy, — to drink in health and happiness from his earnest look, as he gazes strangely upon your pale and shrunken forehead. Your smile even, ghastly with long suffering, disturbs him; there is no interpreter save the heart, between you.

Your parched lips feel strangely, to his flushed, healthful face; and he steps about on tiptoe, at a motion from the nurse, to look at all those rosy-colored medicines upon the table; and he takes your cane from the corner, and passes his hand over the smooth ivory head; and he runs his eye along the wall, from picture to picture, till it rests on one he knows,—a figure in bridal dress, beautiful, almost fond,— and he forgets himself, and says aloud, "There's mamma!"

The nurse puts her finger to her lip; you waken from your doze to see where your eager boy is looking; and your eyes too take in as much as they can of that figure, now shadowy to your fainting vision — doubly shadowy to your fainting heart!

From day to day you sink from life: the physician says the end is not far off; why should it be? There is very little elastic force within you to keep the end away. Madame is called, and your little boy. Your sight is dim, but they whisper that she is beside your bed; and you reach out your hand — both hands. You fancy you hear a sob: a strange sound! It seems as if it came from distant years, — a confused, broken sigh, sweeping over the long stretch of your life; and a sigh from your heart, not audible, answers it.

Your trembling fingers clutch the hand of your little boy, and you drag him toward you, and move your lips as if you would speak to him; and they place his head near you, so that you feel his fine hair brushing your cheek. — My boy, you must love — your mother!

Your other hand feels a quick, convulsive grasp, and something like a tear drops upon your face. Good God! Can it be indeed a tear?

You strain your vision, and a feeble smile flits over your features as you seem to see her figure — the figure of the painting — bending over you; and you feel a bound at your heart, — the same bound that you felt on your bridal morning, the same bound which you used to feel in the spring-time of your life.

——Only one — rich, full bound of the heart: — that is all!

——My cigar was out. I could not have lit it again, if I would. It was wholly burned.

"Aunt Tabithy," said I, as I finished reading, "may I smoke now under your rose-tree?"

Aunt Tabithy, who had laid down her knitting to hear me, smiled, brushed a tear from her old eyes, said, "Yes, Isaac;" and having scratched the back of her head with the disengaged needle, resumed her knitting.

FOURTH REVERIE.

MORNING, NOON, AND EVENING.

MORNING, NOON, AND EVENING.

IT is a spring day under the oaks, the loved oaks of a once cherished home, now, alas! mine no longer.

I had sold the old farm-house, and the groves, and the cool springs where I had bathed my head in the heats of summer; and with the first warm days of May they were to pass from me forever. Seventy years they had been in the possession of my mother's family; for seventy years they had borne the same name of proprietorship; for seventy years the *Lares* of our country home — often neglected, almost forgotten, yet brightened from time to time by gleams of heart-worship — had held their place in the sweet valley of Elmgrove.

And in this changeful, bustling, American life of ours, seventy years is no child's holiday. The hurry of action and progress may pass over it with quick step, but the footprints are many and deep. You surely will not wonder that it made me sad and thoughtful to break the chain of years that bound to my heart the oaks, the hills, the springs, the valley, — and such a valley!

A wild stream runs through it, — large enough to

make a river for English landscape,— winding between rich banks, where in summer-time the swallows build their nests, and brood by myriads.

Tall elms rise here and there along the margin, and with their uplifted arms and leafy spray throw great patches of shade upon the meadow. Old lion-like oaks, too, where the meadow-soil hardens into rolling upland, fasten to the ground with their ridgy roots, and with their gray, scraggy limbs make delicious shelter for the panting workers, or for the herds of August.

Westward of the stream — where I am lying — the banks roll up swiftly into sloping hills covered with groves of oaks, and green pasture lands dotted with mossy rocks. And farther on, where some wood has been swept down, some ten years gone, by the axe, the new growth, heavy with the luxuriant foliage of spring, covers wide spots of the slanting land; while some dead tree in the midst still stretches out its bare arms to the blast, — a solitary mourner over the wreck of its forest brothers.

Eastward, the ridgy bank passes into wavy meadows, upon whose farther edge you see the roofs of an old mansion, with tall chimneys, and taller elm-trees shading it. Beyond, the hills rise gently, and sweep away into wood-crowned heights that are blue with distance. At the upper end of the valley the stream is lost to the eye in a wide swamp wood, which in the autumn-time is covered with a scarlet sheet, blotched here and there by the dark crimson stains of the ash-tops. Farther on, the hills crowd close to the brook, and come down with granite boulders, and scattered birch-trees and beeches, — under which, upon the smoky mornings of May, I have time and again loitered, and thrown my line into the pools, which curl, dark and still, under their tangled roots.

Below, and looking southward, through the openings of the oaks that shade me, I see a broad stretch of meadow, with glimpses of the silver surface of the stream, and of the giant solitary elms, and of some old maple that has yielded to the spring-tides, and now dips its lower boughs in the insidious current; and of clumps of alders, and willow-tufts, — above which even now the black-and-white-coated Bob-o'-Lincoln is wheeling his musical flight, while his quieter mate sits swaying on the topmost twigs.

A quiet road passes within a short distance of me, and crosses the brook by a rude timber bridge; beside the bridge is a broad, glassy pool, shaded by old maples and hickories, where the cattle drink each morning on their way to the hill-pastures. A step or two beyond the stream, a lane branches across the meadows to the mansion with the tall chimneys. I can just remember now the stout, broad-shouldered old gentleman — with his white hat, his long white hair, and his white-headed cane — who built the house, and who farmed the whole valley around me. He is gone long since; and lies in a grave-yard looking upon the sea! The elms that he planted shake their weird arms over the mouldering roofs; and his fruit-garden shows only a battered phalanx of mossy limbs, which will scarce tempt the July marauders.

In the other direction, upon this side the brook, the road is lost to view among the trees; but if I were to follow the windings upon the hill-side, it would bring me shortly upon the old home of my grandfather: there is no pleasure in wandering there now. The woods, that sheltered it from the northern winds, are cut down; the tall cherries, that made the yard one leafy bower, are dead. The cornice is straggling from the eaves; the porch has fallen; the stone chimney is yawning with wide gaps. Within, it is even worse: the floors sway upon the mouldering beams; the doors all sag from their hinges; the rude frescos upon the parlor-wall are peeling off; all is going to decay. — And my grandfather sleeps in a little grave-yard, by the garden-wall.

A lane branches from the country road within a few yards of me, and leads back, along the edge of the meadow, to the homely cottage which has been my special care. Its gray porch and chimney are thrown into rich relief by a grove of oaks that skirts the hill behind it; and the doves are flying uneasily about the open doors of the granary and barns. The morning sun shines pleasantly on the gray group of buildings; and the lowing of the cows, not yet driven a-field, adds to the charming homeliness of the scene. But alas for the poor azalias, and laurels, and vines, that I had put out upon the little knoll before the cottage-door! they are all of them trodden down; only one poor creeper hangs its loose tresses to the lattice, all dishevelled and forlorn!

This by-lane, which opens upon my farm-house, leaves the road in the middle of a grove of oaks; the brown gate swings upon an oak-tree, — the brown gate closes upon an oak-tree. There is a rustic seat, built between two veteran trees that rise from a little hillock near by. Half a century ago, there was a rustic seat on the same hillock, between the same veteran trees. I can trace marks of the old blotches upon the bark, and the scars of the nails upon the scathed trunks. Time and time again it has been renewed. This, the last, was built by my own hands, — a cheerful and a holy duty.

Sixty years ago, they tell me, my grandfather used to loiter here with his gun, while his hounds lay around under the scattered oaks. Now he sleeps, as I said, in the little graveyard yonder, where I can see one or two white tablets glimmering through the foliage. I never knew him; he died, as the brown stone table says, aged twenty-six. Yesterday I climbed the wall that skirts the yard, and plucked a flower from his tomb. I take out now from my pocket-book that flower,— a frail first-blooming violet, — and write upon the slip of paper into which I have thrust its delicate stem: " From my grandfather's tomb: — 1850."

But other feet have trod upon this knoll — far more dear to me. The old neighbors have sometimes told me how they have seen, forty years ago, two rosy-faced girls idling on this spot under the shade, and gathering acorns, and making oak-leaved garlands for their foreheads. Alas, alas! the garlands they wear now are not earthly garlands.

Upon that spot, and upon that rustic seat, I am lying this May morning. I have placed my gun against a tree; my shot-pouch I have hung upon a broken limb. I have thrown my feet upon the bench, and lean against one of the gnarled oaks between which the seat is built. My hat is off; my book and paper are beside me; and my pencil trembles in my fingers as I catch sight of those white marble tablets gleaming through the trees, from the height above me, like beckoning angel-faces. — If they were alive! — two more near and dear friends, in a world where we count friends by units!

It is morning — a bright spring morning under the oaks — these loved oaks of a once cherished home. Last night I slept in yonder mansion under the elms. The cattle going to the pasture are drinking in the pool by the bridge; the boy, who drives them, is making his shrill halloo echo against the hills. The sun has risen fairly over the eastern heights, and shines brightly upon the meadow land, and brightly upon a bend of the brook below me. The birds — the bluebirds sweetest and noisiest of all — are singing over me in the branches. A woodpecker is hammering at a dry limb aloft; and Carlo pricks up his ears and listens, and looks at me, — then stretches out his head upon his paws, in a warm bit of the sunshine, and sleeps.

Morning brings back to me the Past; and the past brings up not only its actualities, not only its events and memories, but — stranger still — what might have been. Every little circumstance, which dawns on the awakened memory, is traced not only to its actual, but to its possible issues.

What a wide world that makes of the Past! — a great and gorgeous, a rich and holy world! Your fancy fills it up artist-like; the darkness is mellowed off into soft shades; the bright spots are veiled in the sweet atmosphere of distance; and fancy and memory together make up a rich dream-land of the past.

And now, as I go on to trace upon paper some of the visions that float across that dream-land of the Morning, I will not — I cannot say, how much comes fancy-wise, and how much from this vaulting memory. Of this the kind reader shall himself be judge.

I.

The Morning.

ISABEL and I — she is my cousin, and is seven years old, and I am ten — are sitting together on the bank of the stream, under an oak-tree that leans half-way over to the water. I am much stronger than she, and taller by a head. I hold in my hands a little alder-rod, with which I am fishing for the roach and minnows that play in the pool below us.

She is watching the cork tossing on the water, or playing with the captured fish that lie upon the bank. She has auburn ringlets that fall down upon her shoulders; and her straw hat lies back upon them, held only by the strip of ribbon that passes under her chin. But the sun does not shine upon her head, for the oak-tree above us is full of leaves; and only here and there a dimple of the sunlight plays upon the pool where I am fishing.

Her eye is hazel, and bright; and now and then she turns it on me with a look of girlish curiosity, as I lift up my rod, — and again in playful menace, as she grasps in her little fingers one of the dead fish, and threatens to throw it back upon the stream. Her little feet hang over the edge of the bank, and from time to time she reaches down to dip her toe in the water, and laughs a girlish laugh of defiance, as I scold her for frightening away the fishes.

"Bella," I say, "what if you should tumble in the river?"

"But I won't."

"Yes, but if you should?"

"Why then you would pull me out."

"But if I would n't pull you out?"

"But I know you would; would n't you, Paul?"

"What makes you think so, Bella?"

"Because you love Bella."

"How do you know I love Bella?"

"Because once you told me so; and because you pick flowers for me that I cannot reach; and because you let me take your rod when you have a fish upon it."

"But that's no reason, Bella."

"Then what is, Paul?"

"I'm sure I don't know, Bella."

A little fish has been nibbling for a long time at the bait; the cork has been bobbing up and down; and now he is fairly hooked, and pulls away toward the bank, and you cannot see the cork.

—"Here, Bella, quick!"—and she springs eagerly to clasp her little hands around the rod. But the fish has dragged it away on the other side of me; and as she reaches farther and farther, she slips, cries "Oh, Paul!"—and falls into the water.

The stream they told us, when we came, was over a man's head: it is surely over little Isabel's. I fling down the rod, and thrusting one hand into the roots that support the overhanging bank, I grasp at her hat as she comes up; but the ribbons give way, and I see the terribly earnest look upon her face as she goes down again. Oh, my mother! thought I, if you were only here!

But she rises again; this time I thrust my hand into her dress, and struggling hard keep her at the top, until I can place my foot down upon a projecting root; and so bracing myself, I drag her to the bank, and having climbed up, take hold of her belt firmly with both hands, and drag her out; and poor Isabel, choked, chilled, and wet, is lying upon the grass.

I commence crying aloud. The workmen in the fields hear me, and come down. One takes Isabel in his arms, and I follow on foot to our uncle's home upon the hill.

—"Oh, my children!" says my mother; and she takes Isabel in her arms; and presently, with dry clothes, and blazing wood-fire, little Bella smiles again I am at my mother's knee.

"I told you so, Paul," says Isabel.—"Aunty, does n't Paul love me?"

"I hope so, Bella," said my mother.

"I know so," said I; and kissed her cheek.

And how did I know it? The boy does not ask, the man does. Oh, the freshness, the honesty, the vigor of a boy's heart! — how the memory of it refreshes like the first gush of spring, or the break of an April shower!

But boyhood has its Pride, as well as its Loves.

My uncle is a tall, hard-faced man. I fear him, when he calls me "child"; I love him, when he calls me "Paul." He is almost always busy with his books; and when I steal into the library-door, as I sometimes do, with a string of fish, or a heaping basket of nuts, to show to him, he looks for a moment curiously at them, sometimes takes them in his fingers, gives them back to me, and turns over the leaves of his book. You are afraid to ask him, if you have not worked bravely; yet you want to do so.

You sidle out softly, and go to your mother. She scarce looks at your little stores; but she draws you to her with her arm, and prints a kiss upon your forehead. Now your tongue is unloosed; that kiss and that action have done it; you will tell what capital luck you have had, and you hold up your tempting trophies; — "Are they not great, mother?" But she is looking in your face, and not at your prize.

"Take them, mother;" and you lay the basket upon her lap.

"Thank you, Paul, I do not wish them; but you must give some to Bella."

And away you go to find laughing, playful cousin Isabel. And we sit down together on the grass, and I pour out my stores between us. "You shall take, Bella, what you wish in your apron, and then, when study-hours are over, we will have such a time down by the big rock in the meadow!"

"But I do not know if papa will let me," says Isabel.

"Bella," I say, "do you love your papa?"

"Yes," says Bella; "why not?"

"Because he is so cold; he does not kiss you, Bella, so often as my mother does; and besides, when he forbids your going away, he does not say, as mother does, 'My little girl will be tired, she had better not go;' but he says only, 'Isabel must not go.' I wonder what makes him talk so?"

"Why, Paul, he is a man, and does n't — At any rate, I love him, Paul. Besides, my mother is sick, you know."

"But Isabel, my mother will be your mother too. Come, Bella, we will go ask her if we may go."

And there I am, the happiest of boys, pleading with the kindest of mothers. And the young heart leans into that mother's heart; — none of the void now that will overtake it like an opening Korah gulf in the years that are to come. It is joyous, full, and running over!

"You may go," she says, "if your uncle is willing."

"But mamma, I am afraid to ask him; I do not believe he loves me."

"Don't say so, Paul;" and she draws you to her side, as if she would supply by her own love the lacking love of a universe.

"Go with your cousin Isabel, and ask him kindly and if he says No, make no reply."

And with courage we go hand-in-hand, and steal in at the library-door. There he sits — I seem to see him now — in the old wainscoted room covered over with books and pictures; and he wears his heavy-rimmed spectacles, and is poring over some big volume full of hard words that are not in any spelling-book. We step up softly, and Isabel lays her little hand upon his arm; and he turns and says, "Well, my little daughter?"

I ask if we may go down to the big rock in the meadow?

He looks at Isabel, and says he is afraid, "we cannot go."

"But why, uncle? It is only a little way, and we will be very careful."

"I am afraid, my children. Do not say any more. You can have the pony, and Tray, and play at home."

"But, uncle" —

"You need say no more, my child."

7*

I pinch the hand of little Isabel, and look in her eye, my own half-filling with tears. I feel that my forehead is flushed, and I hide it behind Bella's tresses, whispering to her at the same time, "Let us go."

"What, sir," says my uncle, mistaking my meaning do you persuade her to disobey?"

Now I am angry, and say blindly, "No, sir, I did n't! And then my rising pride will not let me say that I wished only Isabel should go out with me.

Bella cries; and I shrink out, and am not easy until I have run to bury my head in my mother's bosom. Alas! pride cannot always find such covert. There will be times when it will harass you strangely; when it will peril friendships — will sever old, standing intimacy; and then — no resource but to feed on its own bitterness. Hateful pride! to be conquered as a man would conquer an enemy, or it will make whirlpools in the current of your affections, — nay, turn the whole tide of the heart into rough and unaccustomed channels.

But boyhood has its Grief too, apart from Pride.

You love the old dog Tray; and Bella loves him as well as you. He is a noble old fellow, with shaggy hair and long ears, and big paws that he will put up into your hand, if you ask him. And he never gets angry when you play with him, and tumble him over in the long grass, and pull his silken ears. Sometimes, to be sure, he will open his mouth as if he would bite, but when he gets your hand fairly in his jaws, he will scarce leave the print of his teeth upon it. He will swim, too, bravely, and bring ashore all the sticks you throw upon the water; and when you fling a stone to tease him, he swims round and round, and whines and looks sorry that e cannot find it.

He will carry a heaping basket full of nuts, too, in his mouth, and never spill one of them; and when you come out to your uncle's home in the spring, after staying a whole winter in the town, he knows you — old Tray does! And he leaps upon you, and lays his paws on your shoulder, and licks your face, and is almost as glad to see you as cousin Bella herself. And when you put Bella on his back for a ride, he only pretends to bite her little feet; but he would n't do it for the world. Aye, Tray is a noble old dog!

But one summer the farmers say that some of their sheep are killed, and that the dogs have worried them; and one of them comes to talk with my uncle about it.

But Tray never worried sheep; you know he never did; and so does nurse; and so does Bella; for in the spring she had a pet lamb, and Tray never worried ittle Fidèle.

And one or two of the dogs that belong to the neighbors are shot; though nobody knows who shot them, and you have great fears about poor Tray; and try to keep him at home, and fondle him more than ever. But

Tray will sometimes wander off; till, finally, one afternoon he comes back whining piteously, and with his shoulder all bloody.

Little Bella cries loud; and you almost cry, as nurse dresses the wound; and poor old Tray whines very sadly. You pat his head, and Bella pats him; and you sit down together by him on the floor of the porch, and bring a rug for him to lie upon, and try and tempt him with a little milk; and Bella brings a piece of cake for him, — but he will eat nothing. You sit up till very late, long after Bella has gone to bed, patting his head, and wishing you could do something for poor Tray; but he only licks your hand, and whines more piteously than ever.

In the morning you dress early, and hurry downstairs; but Tray is not lying on the rug; and you run through the house to find him, and whistle and call — Tray! Tray! At length you see him lying in his old place out by the cherry-tree, and you run to him, — but he does not start; and you lean down to pat him, — but he is cold, and the dew is wet upon him. Poor Tray is dead!

You take his head upon your knees, and pat again those glossy ears, and cry; but you cannot bring him to 'ife. And Bella comes and cries with you. You can hardly bear to have him put in the ground; but uncle says he must be buried. So one of the workmen digs a grave under the cherry-tree where he died, — a deep grave; and they round it over with earth, and smooth the sods upon it; — even now I can trace Tray's grave.

You and Bella together put up a little slab for a tombstone; and she hangs flowers upon it, and ties them there with a bit of ribbon. You can scarce play all that day; and afterward, many weeks later, when you are rambling over the fields, or lingering by the brook, throwing off sticks into the eddies, you think of old Tray's shaggy coat, and of his big paw, and of his honest eye; and the memory of your boyish grief comes upon you, and you say, with tears, " Poor Tray!" And Bella too, in her sad, sweet tones, says, " Poor old Tray, he is dead!"

School-Days.

THE morning was cloudy and threatened rain; besides, it was autumn weather, and the winds were getting harsh, and rustling among the tree-tops, that shaded the house, most dismally. I did not dare to listen. If indeed I were to stay by the bright fires of home, and gather the nuts as they fell, and pile up the falling leaves, to make great bonfires with Ben and the rest of the boys, I should have liked to listen, and would have braved the dismal morning with the cheerfullest of them all. For it would have been a capital time to light a fire in the little oven we had built under the wall; it would have been so pleasant to warm our fingers at it, and to roast the great russets on the flat stones that made the top.

But this was not in store for me. I had bid the town-boys good-bye the day before; my trunk was all packed I was to go away — to school. The little oven would go to ruin — I knew it would. I was to leave my home. I was to bid my mother good-bye, and Lilly, and Isabel, and all the rest; and was to go away from them so far that I should only know what they were all doing — in letters. It *was* sad. And then to have the clouds come over on that morning, and the winds sigh so dismally; oh, it was too bad, I thought!

It comes back to me, as I lie here this bright spring morning, as if it were only yesterday. I remember that the pigeons skulked under the eaves of the carriage-house, and did not sit, as they used to do in summer, upon the ridge; and the chickens huddled together about the stable-doors as if they were afraid of the cold autumn. And in the garden the white hollyhocks stood shivering, and bowed to the wind, as if their time had come. The yellow muskmelons showed plain among the frost-bitten vines, and looked cold and uncomfortable.

—— Then they were all so kind in-doors! The

cook made such nice things for my breakfast, because little master was going; Lilly *would* give me her seat by the fire, and would put her lump of sugar in my cup; and my mother looked so smiling and so tenderly, that I thought I loved her more than I ever did before. Little Ben was so gay too; and wanted me to take his jackknife, if I wished it, — though he knew that I had a bran new one in my trunk. The old nurse slipped a little purse into my hand, tied up with a green ribbon,— with money in it,— and told me not to show it to Ben or Lilly.

And cousin Isabel, who was there on a visit, would come to stand by my chair when my mother was talking to me, and put her hand in mine, and look up into my face; but she did not say a word. I thought it was very odd; and yet it did not seem odd to me that I could say nothing to her. I dare say we felt alike.

At length Ben came running in, and said the coach had come; and there, sure enough, out of the window we saw it, — a bright yellow coach, with four white horses, and bandboxes all over the top, with a great pile of trunks behind. Ben said it was a grand coach, and that he should like a ride in it; and the old nurse came to the door, and said I should have a capital time; but somehow I doubted if the nurse was talking honestly. I believe she gave me an honest kiss though — and such a hug!

But it was nothing to my mother's. Tom told me to be a man, and study like a Trojan; but I was not thinking about study then. There was a tall boy in the coach, and I was ashamed to have him see me cry; so I did n't at first. But I remember, as I looked back and saw little Isabel run out into the middle of the street to see the coach go off, and the curls floating behind her as the wind freshened, I felt my heart leaping into my throat, and the water coming into my eyes,— and how just then I caught sight of the tall boy glancing at me, — and how I tried to turn it off by looking to see if I could button up my great-coat a great deal lower down than the button-holes went.

But it was of no use. I put my head out of the coach-window, and looked back as the little figure of Isabel faded, and then the house, and the trees; and the tears did come; and I smuggled my handkerchief outside without turning, so that I could wipe my eyes before the tall boy should see me. They say that these shadows of morning fade as the sun brightens into noonday; but they are very dark shadows for all that!

Let the father or the mother think long before they send away their boy, — before they break the home ties that make a web of infinite fineness and soft silken meshes around his heart, and toss him aloof into the boy-world, where he must struggle up, amid bickerings and quarrels, into his age of youth! There are boys indeed with little fineness in the texture of their hearts, and with little delicacy of soul, to whom the school in a distant village is but a vacation from home, and with whom a return revives all those grosser affections which alone existed before; just as there are plants which will bear all exposure without the wilting of a leaf, and will return to the hot-house life as strong and as hopeful as ever. But there are others, to whom the severance from the prattle of sisters, the indulgent fondness of a mother, and the unseen influences of the home altar, gives a shock that lasts forever; it is wrenching with cruel hand what will bear but little roughness; and the sobs with which the adieus are said are sobs that may come back in the after-years strong and steady and terrible.

God have mercy on the boy who learns to sob early! Condemn it as sentiment, if you will; talk as you will of the fearlessness and strength of the boy's heart, — yet there belong to many tenderly strung chords of affection which give forth low and gentle music that consoles and ripens the ear for all the harmonies of life. These chords a little rude and unnatural tension will break, and break forever. Watch your boy then, if so be he will bear the strain; try his nature if it be rude or delicate; and if delicate, in God's name, do not, as you value your peace and his, breed a harsh youth-spirit in him that shall take pride in subjugating and forgetting the delicacy and richness of his finer affections!

—— I see now, looking into the past, the troops of boys who were scattered in the great play-ground as the coach drove up at night. The school was in a tall, stately building, with a high cupola on the top, where thought I would like to go up. The schoolmaster, they told me at home, was kind; he said he hoped I would be a good boy, and patted me on the head; but he did not pat me as my mother used to do. Then there was a woman whom they called the Matron, who had a great many ribbons in her cap, and who shook my hand, — but so stiffly, that I did n't dare to look up in her face.

One boy took me down to see the school-room, which was in the basement, and the walls were all mouldy, I remember; and when we passed a certain door, he said — there was the dungeon; — how I felt! I hated that boy; but I believe he is dead now. Then the matron took me up to my room, — a little corner-room, with two beds and two windows, and a red table, and closet; and my chum was about my size, and wore a queer roundabout jacket with big bell buttons; and he called the schoolmaster "Old Crikey," and kept me awake half the night, telling me how he whipped the scholars, and how they played tricks upon him. I thought my chum was a very uncommon boy.

For a day or two the lessons were easy, and it was sport to play with so many "fellows." But soon I began to feel lonely at night, after I had gone to bed. I used to wish I could have my mother come and kiss me after school, too, I wished I could step in and tell Isabel how bravely I had got my lessons. When I told my chum this, he laughed at me, and said that was no place for "homesick, white-livered chaps." I wondered if my chum had any mother.

We had spending-money once a week, with which we used to go down to the village store, and club our funds together to make great pitchers of lemonade. Some boys would have money besides, though it was against the rules; and one, I recollect, showed us a five-dollar bill in his wallet, and we all thought he must be very rich.

We marched in procession to the village church on Sundays. There were two long benches in the galleries, reaching down the sides of the meeting-house, and on these we sat. At the first I was among the smallest boys, and took a place close to the wall against the pulpit; but afterward, as I grew bigger, I was promoted to the lower end of the first bench. This I never liked, because it was close by one of the ushers, and because it brought me next to some countrywomen who wore stiff bonnets, and ate fennel, and sung with the choir But there was a little black-eyed girl, who sat over behind the choir, that I thought handsome. I used to look at her very often, but was careful she should never catch my eye.

There was another down below, in a corner-pew, who was pretty, and who wore a hat in the winter trimmed with fur. Half the boys in the school said they would marry her some day or other. One's name was Jane, and that of the other Sophia; which we thought pretty names, and cut them on the ice in skating-time. But I did n't think either of them so pretty as Isabel.

Once a teacher whipped me. I bore it bravely in the school; but afterward, at night, when my chum was asleep, I sobbed bitterly as I thought of Isabel, and Ben, and my mother, and how much they loved me; and laying my face in my hands, I sobbed myself to sleep. In the morning I was calm enough : it was another of the heart-ties broken, though I did not know it then. It lessened the old attachment to home, because that home could neither protect me nor soothe me with its sympathies Memory, indeed, freshened and grew strong, but strong in bitterness and in regrets. The boy whose love you cannot feed by daily nourishment will find pride self-indulgence, and an iron purpose coming in to furnish other supply for the soul that is in him. If he cannot shoot his branches into the sunshine, he will become acclimated to the shadow, and indifferent to such stray gleams of sunshine as his fortune may vouchsafe.

Hostilities would sometimes threaten between the school and the village boys; but they usually passed off with such loud and harmless explosions as belong to the wars of our small politicians. The village champions were a hatter's apprentice and a thick-set fellow who worked in a tannery. We prided ourselves especially on one stout boy, who wore a sailor's monkey-jacket. I cannot but think how jaunty that stout boy looked in that jacket, and what an Ajax cast there was to his countenance! It certainly did occur to me to compare him with William Wallace, (Miss Porter's William Wallace,) and I thought how I would have liked to have seen a tussle between them. Of course we, who were small boys, limited ourselves to indignant remarks, and thought "we should like to see them do it"; and prepared clubs from the wood-shed, after a model suggested by a New-York boy who had seen the clubs of the policemen.

There was one scholar — poor Leslie — who had friends in some foreign country, and who occasionally received letters bearing a foreign postmark. What an extraordinary boy that was; what astonishing letters what extraordinary parents! I wondered if I should ever receive a letter from "foreign parts." I wondered if I should ever write one; — but this was too much, too absurd! As if I, Paul, wearing a blue jacket with gilt buttons, and number-four boots, should ever visit those countries spoken of in the geographies and by learned travellers! No, no; this was too extravagant; but I knew what I would do if I lived to come of age, — and I vowed that I would — I would go to New York!

Number Seven was the hospital, and forbidden ground; we had all of us a sort of horror of Number Seven. A boy died there once, and oh! how he moaned; and what a time there was when the father came!

A scholar by the name of Tom Belton, who wore linsey gray, made a dam across a little brook by the school and whittled out a saw-mill that actually sawed: he had genius. I expected to see him before now at the head of American mechanics, but I learn with pain that he is keeping a grocery-store.

At the close of all the terms we had exhibitions, to which all the townspeople came, and among them the black-eyed Jane, and the pretty Sophia with fur around her hat. My great triumph was when I had the part of one of Pizarro's chieftains, the evening before I left the school. How I did look! I had a moustache put on with burnt cork, and whiskers very bushy indeed; and I had the militia coat of an ensign in the town company, with the skirts pinned up; and a short sword, very dull and crooked, which belonged to an old gentleman who was said to have got it from some privateer's-man, who was said to have taken it from some great British admiral in the old wars; and the way I carried

THE MORNING.

that sword upon the platform, and the way I jerked it out when it came to my turn to say, "Battle! battle!— then death to the armed, and chains for the defenceless!"— was tremendous.

The morning after, in our dramatic hats,— black felt, with turkey feathers,— we took our place upon the top of the coach to leave the school. The head master, in green spectacles, came out to shake hands with us,— a very awful shaking of hands. Poor gentleman! he is in his grave now.

We gave three loud hurrahs "for the old school," as the coach started; and upon the top of the hill that overlooks the village we gave another round, and still another for the crabbed old fellow whose apples we had so often stolen. I wonder if old Bulkeley is living yet?

As we got on under the pine-trees, I recalled the image of the black-eyed Jane, and of the other little girl in the corner-pew, and thought how I would come back after the college-days were over,— a man, with a beaver hat and a cane, and with a splendid barouche; and how I would take the best chamber at the inn, and astonish the old schoolmaster by giving him a familiar tap on the shoulder; and how I would be the admiration and the wonder of the pretty girl in the fur-trimmed hat! Alas! how our thoughts outrun our deeds.

For long — long years I saw no more of my old school; and when at length the new view came, great changes, crashing like tornadoes, had swept over my path. I thought no more of startling the villagers or astonishing the black-eyed girl. No, no! I was content to slip quietly through the little town, with only a tear or two, as I recalled the dead ones and mused upon the emptiness of life.

The Sea.

As I look back, boyhood with its griefs and cares vanishes into the proud stateliness of youth. The ambition and the rivalries of the college-life, its first boastful importance as knowledge begins to dawn on the wakened mind, and the ripe and enviable complacency of its senior dignity, — all scud over my memory like this morning breeze along the meadows, and like that, too, bear upon their wing a chillness as of distant ice-banks.

Ben has grown almost to manhood; Lilly is living in a distant home; and Isabel is just blooming into that sweet age where womanly dignity waits her beauty, — an age that sorely puzzles one who has grown up beside her, making him slow of tongue, but very quick of heart!

As for the rest — let us pass on.

The sea is around me. The last headlands have gone down under the horizon, like the city steeples, as you lose yourself in the calm of the country, or like the great thoughts of genius, as you slip from the pages of poets into your own quiet reverie

The waters skirt me right and left; there is nothing but water before, and only water behind. Above me are sailing clouds, or the blue vault, which we call, with childish license, heaven. The sails white and full, like helping friends, are pushing me on; and night and day are distent with the winds which come and go — none know whence, and none know whither. A land-bird flutters aloft, weary with long flying, and lost in a world where are no forests but the careening masts, and no foliage but the drifts of spray. It cleaves a while to the smooth spars, still urged by some homeward yearning; it bears off in the face of the wind, and sinks and rises over the angry waters, until its strength is gone, and the blue waves gather the poor flutterer to their cold and glassy bosom.

All the morning I see nothing beyond me but the waters, or a tossing company of dolphins; all the noon, unless some white sail, like a ghost, stalks the horizon, there is still nothing but the rolling seas; all the evening, after the sun has grown big and sunk under the water-line, and the moon risen white and cold to glimmer across the tops of the surging ocean, there is nothing but the sea and the sky to lead off thought, or to crush it with their greatness.

Hour after hour, as I sit in the moonlight upon the taffrail, the great waves gather far back and break, — and gather nearer, and break louder, — and gather again, and roll down swift and terrible under the creaking ship, and heave it up lightly upon their swelling surge, and drop it gently to their seething and yeasty cradle, like an infant in the swaying arms of a mother, or like a shadowy memory upon the billows of manly thought.

Conscience wakes in the silent nights of ocean; life lies open like a book, and spreads out as level as the sea. Regrets and broken resolutions chase over the soul like swift-winged night-birds; and all the unsteady heights and the wastes of action lift up distinct and clear from the uneasy but limpid depths of memory.

Yet within this floating world I am upon, sympathies are narrowed down; they cannot range, as upon the land, over a thousand objects. You are strangely attracted toward some frail girl, whose pallor has now given place to the rich bloom of the sea-life. You listen eagerly to the chance-snatches of a song from below in the long morning watch. You love to see her small feet tottering on the unsteady deck; and you love greatly to aid her steps, and feel her weight upon your arm, as the ship lurches to a heavy sea.

Hopes and fears knit together pleasantly upon the ocean. Each day seems to revive them; your morning salutation is like a welcome after absence upon the shore, and each "good-night" has the depth and fulness of a land "farewell." And beauty grows upon the ocean; you cannot certainly say that the face of the fair girl-voyager is prettier than that of Isabel; oh, no! but you are certain that you cast innocent and honest glances upon her, as you steady her walk upon the deck, far oftener than at first; and ocean life and sympathy makes her kind; she does not resent your rudeness one half so stoutly as she might upon the shore.

She will even linger of an evening — pleading first with the mother, and, standing beside you, — her white hand not very far from yours upon the rail, — look down where the black ship flings off with each plunge whole garlands of emeralds; or she will look up (thinking perhaps you are looking the same way) into the skies in search of some stars — which were her neighbors at home. And bits of old tales will come up as if they rode upon the ocean quietude; and fragments of half forgotten poems, tremulously uttered, either by reason of the rolling of the ship, or some accidental touch of that white hand.

But ocean has its storms, when fear will make strange and holy companionship; and even here my memory shifts swiftly and suddenly.

———— It is a dreadful night. The passengers are clustered, trembling, below. Every plank shakes; and the oak ribs groan as if they suffered with their toil. The hands are all aloft; the captain is forward shouting to the mate in the cross-trees, and I am clinging to one of the stanchions by the binnacle. The ship is pitching madly, and the waves are toppling up sometimes as high as the yard-arm, and then dipping away with a whirl under our keel, that makes every timber in the vessel quiver. The thunder is roaring like a thousand cannons; and at the moment the sky is cleft with a stream of fire that glares over the tops of the waves, and glistens on the wet decks and the spars, — lighting up all so plain, that I can see the men's faces in the main-top, and catch glimpses of the reefers on the yard-arm, clinging like death; — then all is horrible darkness.

The spray spits angrily against the canvas; the waves crash against the weather-bow like mountains; the wind howls through the rigging, or, as a gasket gives way, the sail, bellying to leeward, splits like a crack of a musket. I hear the captain in the lulls screaming out orders; and the mate in the rigging screaming them over, until the lightning comes, and the thunder, deadening their voices as if they were chirping sparrows.

In one of the flashes I see a hand upon the yard-arm lose his foothold as the ship gives a plunge; but his arms are clenched around the spar. Before I can see any more, the blackness comes, and the thunder, with a crash that half deafens me. I think I hear a low cry, as the mutterings die away in the distance; and at the next flash of lightning, which comes in an instant, I see upon the top of one of the waves alongside the poor reefer who has fallen. The lightning glares upon his face.

But he has caught at a loose bit of running rigging as he fell; and I see it slipping off the coil upon the deck. I shout madly, "Man overboard!" and catch the rope, when I can see nothing again. The sea is too high, and the man too heavy for me. I shout, and shout, and shout, and feel the perspiration starting in great beads from my forehead as the line slips through my fingers.

Presently the captain feels his way aft and takes hold with me; and the cook comes as the coil is nearly spent, and we pull together upon him. It is desperate work for the sailor; for the ship is drifting at a prodigious rate; but he clings like a dying man.

By-and-by at a flash we see him on a crest two oars' lengths away from the vessel.

"Hold on, my man!" shouts the captain.

"For God's sake, be quick!" says the poor fellow and he goes down in the trough of the sea. We pul the harder, and the captain keeps calling to him to keep up courage and hold strong. But in the hush we can near him say,—"I can't hold out much longer; I'm most gone!"

Presently we have brought the man where we can

lay hold of him, and are only waiting for a good lift of the sea to bring him up, when the poor fellow groans out, — "It's of no use — I can't — good-bye!" And a wave tosses the end of the rope clean upon the bulwarks.

At the next flash I see him going down under the water.

I grope my way below, sick and faint at heart; and wedging myself into my narrow berth, I try to sleep. But the thunder and the tossing of the ship, and the face of the drowning man as he said good-bye, peering at me from every corner, will not let me sleep.

Afterward come quiet seas, over which we boom along, leaving in our track at night a broad path of phosphorescent splendor. The sailors bustle around the decks as if they had lost no comrade; and the voyagers, losing the pallor of fear, look out earnestly for the land.

At length my eyes rest upon the coveted fields of Britain; and in a day more the bright face, looking out beside me, sparkles at sight of the sweet cottages which lie along the green Essex shores. Broad-sailed yachts, looking strangely yet beautifully, glide upon the waters of the Thames like swans; black, square-rigged colliers from the Tyne lie grouped in sooty cohorts; and heavy, three-decked Indiamen — of which I had read in storybooks — drift slowly down with the tide. Dingy steamers with white pipes and with red pipes, whiz past us to the sea; and now my eye rests on the great palace of Greenwich; I see the wooden-legged pensioners smoking under the palace-walls, and above them upon the hill — as Heaven is true — that old fabulous Greenwich, the great centre of school-boy Longitude.

Presently, from under a cloud of murky smoke heaves up the vast dome of St. Paul's, and the tall Column of the Fire, and the white turrets of London Tower. Our ship glides through the massive dock-gates, and is moored amid the forest of masts which bears golden fruit for Britons.

That night I sleep far away from "the old school," and far away from the valley of Hillfarm. Long and late I toss upon my bed, with sweet visions in my mind of London Bridge, and Temple Bar, and Jane Shore, and Falstaff, and Prince Hal, and King Jamie. And when at length I fall asleep, my dreams are very pleasant, but they carry me across the ocean, away from the ship, away from London, away even from the fair voyager, — to the old oaks, and to the brooks, and — to thy side, sweet Isabel!

The Father-Land.

THERE is a great contrast between the easy *déshabille* of the ocean life and the prim attire and conventional spirit of the land In the first there are but few to please, and these few are known, and they know us, upon the shore there is a world to humor, and a world of strangers. In a brilliant drawing-room looking out upon the site of old Charing Cross, and upon the one-armed Nelson standing aloft at his coil of rope, I take leave of the fair voyager of the sea. Her white *négligé* has given place to silks; and the simple, careless *coiffe* of the ocean is replaced by the rich dressing of a *modiste*. Yet her face has the same bloom upon it; and her eye sparkles, as it seems to me, with a higher pride; and her little hand has, I think, a tremulous quiver in it (I am sure my own has) as I bid her adieu, and take up the trail of my wanderings into the heart of England.

Abuse her as we will, — pity her starving peasantry as we may, — smile at her court pageantry as much as we like, — old England is dear old England still. Her cottage-homes, her green fields, her castles, her blazing firesides, her church-spires are as old as song; and by song and story we inherit them in our hearts. This joyous boast was, I remember, upon my lip as I first trod upon the rich meadow of Runnymede, and recalled that Great Charter wrested from the king, which made the first stepping-stone toward the bounties of our western freedom.

It is a strange feeling that comes over the western Saxon as he strolls first along the green by-lanes of

England, and scents the hawthorn in its April bloom, and lingers at some quaint stile to watch the rooks wheeling and cawing around some lofty elm-tops, and traces the carved gables of some old country mansion that lies in their shadow, and hums some fragment of charming English poesy that seems made for the scene This is not sight-seeing nor travel; it is dreaming sweet dreams that are fed with the old life of Books.

I wander on, fearing to break the dream by a swift step; and, winding and rising between the blooming hedgerows, I come presently to the sight of some sweet valley below me, where a thatched hamlet lies sleeping in the April sun as quietly as the dead lie in history; no sound reaches me save the occasional clink of the smith's hammer, or the hedgeman's billhook, or the ploughman's "ho-tup!" from the hills. At evening, listening to the nightingale, I stroll wearily into some close-nestled village that I had seen long ago from a rolling height. It is far away from the great lines of travel; and the children stop their play to have a look at me, and the rosy-faced girls peep from behind half-opened doors.

Standing apart, and with a bench on either side of the entrance, is the inn of the Eagle and the Falcon,— which guardian birds some native Dick Tinto has pictured upon the swinging sign-board at the corner. The hostess is half ready to embrace me, and treats me like a prince in disguise. She shows me through the tap-room into a little parlor with white curtains, and with neatly framed prints of the old patriarchs. Here, alone, beside a brisk fire kindled with furze, I watch the white flame leaping playfully through the black lumps of coal, and enjoy the best fare of the Eagle and the Falcon. If too late or too early for her garden-stock, the hostess bethinks herself of some small pot of jelly in an out-of-the-way cupboard of the house, and setting it tempt-ingly in her prettiest dish, she coyly slips it upon the white cloth, with a modest regret that it is no better, and a little evident satisfaction that it is so good.

I muse for an hour before the glowing fire, as quiet as the cat that has come in to bear me company; and at bedtime I find sheets as fresh as the air of the mountains.

At another time, and many months later, I am walk-ing under a wood of Scottish firs. It is near nightfall, and the fir-tops are swaying, and sighing hoarsely in the cool wind of the Northern Highlands. There is none of the smiling landscape of England about me; and the crags of Edinburgh and Castle Stirling, and sweet Perth, in its silver valley, are far to the southward. The larches of Athol and Bruar Water, and that highland gem, Dunkeld, are passed. I am tired with a morn ing's tramp over Culloden Moor; and from the edge of the wood there stretch before me, in the cool gray twi light, broad fields of heather. In the middle there rise against the night-sky the turrets of a castle ; it is Castle Cawdor, where King Duncan was murdered by Macbeth.

The sight of it lends a spur to my weary step ; and emerging from the wood, I bound over the springy heather. In an hour I clamber a broken wall, and come under the frowning shadows of the castle. The ivy clambers up here and there, and shakes its uncropped branches and its dried berries over the heavy portal. I cross the moat, and my step makes the chains of the drawbridge rattle. All is kept in the old state; only in lieu of the warder's horn I pull at the warder's bell. The echoes ring and die in the stone courts ; but there is no one astir, nor is there a light at any of the castle-windows. I ring again and the echoes come and blend with the rising night-wind that sighs around the turrets as they sighed that night of murder. I fancy — it must be a fancy — that I hear an owl scream ; I am sure that I hear the crickets cry.

I sit down upon the green bank of the moat ; a little dark water lies in the bottom. The walls rise from it gray and stern in the deepening shadows. I hum chance passages of Macbeth, listening for the echoes,— echoes from the wall, and echoes from that far away time when I stole the first reading of the tragic story.

"Didst thou not hear a noise?
I heard the owl scream, and the crickets cry.
Did not you speak?
When?
Now.
As I descended?
Ay.
Hark!"

And the sharp echo comes back — "hark!" And at dead of night, in the thatched cottage under the castle-walls, where a dark-faced Gaelic woman in plaid turban is my hostess, I wake, startled by the wind, and my trembling lips say involuntarily — "hark!"

Again, three months later, I am in the sweet county of Devon. Its valleys are like emerald; its threads of waters, stretched over the fields by their provident husbandry, glisten in the broad glow of summer like skeins of silk. A bland old farmer, of the true British stamp, is my host. On market-days he rides over to the old town of Totness in a trim, black farmer's cart; and he wears glossy topped boots and a broad-brimmed white hat. I take a vast deal of pleasure in listening to his honest, straightforward talk about the improvements of the day and the state of the nation. I sometimes get upon one of his nags, and ride off with him over his fields, or visit the homes of the laborers, which show their gray roofs in every charming nook of the landscape. At the parish-church I doze against the high pew-backs as I listen to the seesaw tones of the drawling curate; and in my half-wakeful moments the withered holly-sprigs (not removed since Easter) grow upon my vision into Christmas boughs, and preach sermons to me of the days of old.

Sometimes I wander far over the hills into a neighboring park, and spend hours on hours under the sturdy oaks, watching the sleek fallow deer gazing at me with their soft, liquid eyes. The squirrels, too, play above me with their daring leaps, utterly careless of my presence, and the pheasants whir away from my very feet.

On one of these random strolls, — I remember it very well, — when I was idling along, thinking of the broad reach of water that lay between me and that old forest home, and beating off the daisy heads with my cane, I heard the tramp of horses coming up one of the forest avenues. The sound was unusual, for the family, I had been told, was still in town, and no right of way lay through the park. There they were, however; — I was sure it must be the family, from the careless way in which they came sauntering up.

First there was a noble hound that came bounding toward me, gazed a moment, and turned to watch the approach of the little cavalcade. Next was an elderly gentleman mounted upon a spirited hunter, attended by a boy of some dozen years, who managed his pony with a grace that is a part of the English boy's education. Then followed two older lads, and a travelling phaeton in which sat a couple of elderly ladies. But what most drew my attention was a girlish figure that rode beyond the carriage upon a sleek-limbed gray. There was something in the easy grace of her attitude and the rich glow that lit up her face — heightened, as it was, by the little black riding-cap relieved with a single flowing plume — that kept my eye. It was strange, but I thought that I had seen such a figure before, and such a face, and such an eye; and as I made the ordinary salutation of a stranger, and caught her smile, I could have sworn that it was she — my fair companion of the ocean. The truth flashed upon me in a moment. She was to visit, she had told me, a friend in the south of England; — and this was the friend's home; and one of the ladies in the carriage was her mother, and one of the lads the school-boy brother who had teased her on the sea.

I recall now perfectly her frank manner as she ungloved her hand to bid me welcome. I strolled beside them to the steps. Old Devon had suddenly renewed its beauties for me. I had much to tell her of the little outlying nooks which my wayward feet had led me to; and she — as much to ask. My stay with the bland old farmer lengthened; and two days' hospitalities at the Park ran over into three, and four. There was hard galloping down those avenues; and new strolls, not at all lonely, under the sturdy oaks. The long summer twilight of England used to find a very happy fellow lingering on the garden-terrace, looking now at the rookery, where the belated birds quarrelled for a resting-place, and now down the long forest vista, gray with distance, and closed with the white spire of Madbury church.

English country life gains fast upon one — very fast; and it is not so easy as in the drawing-room of Charing Cross, to say — adieu! But it is said — very sadly said; for God only knows how long it is to last. And as I rode slowly down toward the lodge after my leave-taking, I turned back again, and again, and again. I thought I saw her standing still upon the terrace, though it was almost dark; and I thought — it could hardly have been an illusion — that I saw something white waving from her hand.

Her name — as if I could forget it — was Caroline; her mother called her Carry. I wondered how it would seem for me to call her Carry! I tried it: it sounded well. I tried it over and over, until I came too near the lodge. There I threw a half-crown to the woman who opened the gate for me. She curtsied low, and said, "God bless you, sir!"

I liked her for it; I would have given a guinea for it; and that night — whether it was the old woman's benediction or the waving scarf upon the terrace, I do not know, but — there was a charm upon my thought and my hope, as if an angel had been near me.

It passed away, though, in my dreams; for I dreamed that I saw the sweet face of Bella in an English park, and that she wore a black velvet riding-cap with a plume; and I came up to her and murmured, — very sweetly, I thought, — "Carry, dear Carry!" and she started, looked sadly at me, and turned away. I ran after her to kiss her as I did when she sat upon my mother's lap, on the day when she came near drowning I longed to tell her, as I did then, I *do* love you. But she turned her tearful face upon me, I dreamed; and then — I saw no more.

A Roman Girl.

—— I REMEMBER the very words, — "*Non parlo Francese, Signore,*— I do not speak French, Signor," said the stout lady; "but my daughter, perhaps, will understand you."

And she called, "*Enrica! Enrica! venite, subito! c' è un forestiere.*"

And the daughter came, her light-brown hair falling carelessly over her shoulders, her rich hazel eye twinkling and full of life, the color coming and going upon her transparent cheek, and her bosom heaving with her quick step. With one hand she put back the scattered locks that had fallen over her forehead, while she laid the other gently upon the arm of her mother, and asked in that sweet music of the south, "*Cosa volete, mamma?*"

It was the prettiest picture I had seen in many a day; and this notwithstanding I was in Rome, and had come that very morning from the Palace of Borghese.

The stout lady was my hostess, and Enrica — so fair, so young, so unlike in her beauty to other Italian beauties — was my landlady's daughter. The house was one of those tall houses — very, very old — which stand along the eastern side of the Corso, looking out upon the Piazzo di Colonna. The staircases were very tall and dirty, and they were narrow and dark. Four flights of stone steps led up to the corridor where they lived. A little trap was in the door, and there was a bell-rope, at the least touch of which I was almost sure to hear tripping feet run along the stone floor within, and then to see the trap thrown slyly back, and those deep hazel eyes looking out upon me; and then the door would open, and along the corridor, under the daughter's guidance, (until I had learned the way,) I passed to my Roman home. I was a long time learning the way.

My chamber looked out upon the Corso, and I could catch from it a glimpse of the top of the tall column of Antoninus, and of a fragment of the palace of the Governor. My parlor, which was separated from the apartments of the family by a narrow corridor, looked upon a small court hung around with balconies. From the upper one a couple of black-eyed girls are occasionally looking out, and they can almost read the title of my book when I sit by the window. Below are three or four blooming *ragazze*, who are dark-eyed, and have Roman luxuriance of hair. The youngest is a friend of our Enrica, and is of course frequently looking up, with all the innocence in the world, to see if Enrica may be looking out.

Night after night a bright blaze glows upon my hearth, of the alder fagots which they bring from the Alban hills. Night after night, too, the family come in, to aid my blundering speech, and to enjoy the rich sparkling of my fagot-fire. Little Cesare, a dark-faced Italian boy, takes up his position with pencil and slate, and draws by the light of the blaze genii and castles. The old one-eyed teacher of Enrica lays his snuffbox upon the table, and his handkerchief across his lap, and with his spectacles upon his nose, and his big fingers on the lesson, runs through the French tenses of the verb *amare*. The father, a sallow-faced, keen-eyed man with true Italian visage, sits with his arms upon the elbows of his chair, and talks of the Pope, or of the weather. A spruce count, from the Marches of Ancona, wears heavy watch-seal, and reads Dante with *furore*. The mother, with arms akimbo, looks proudly upon her daughter, and counts her, as well she may, a gem among the Roman beauties.

The table was round, with the fire blazing on one side; there was scarce room for but three upon the other. Signor *il maestro* was one; then Enrica; and next — how well I remember it — came myself. For I could sometimes help Enrica to a word of French; and far oftener she could help me to a word of Italian. Her face was rich and full of feeling; I used greatly to love to watch the puzzled expressions that passed over her forehead as the sense of some hard phrase escaped her; and, better still, to see the happy smile as she caught at a glance the thought of some old scholastic Frenchman, and transferred it into the liquid melody of her speech.

She had seen just sixteen summers, and only that very autumn was escaped from the thraldom of a convent upon the skirts of Rome. She knew nothing of life but the life of feeling, and all thoughts of happiness lay as yet in her childish hopes. It was pleasant to look upon her face, and it was still more pleasant to listen to that sweet Roman voice. What a rich flow of superlatives and endearing diminutives from those vermilion lips! Who would not have loved the study; and who would not have loved — without meaning it — the teacher?

In those days I did not linger long at the tables of Dame Pietro in the Via Condotti, but would hurry back to my little Roman parlor — the fire was so pleasant

And it was so pleasant to greet Enrica with her mother even before the one-eyed *maestro* had come in; and it was pleasant to unfold the book between us, and to lay my hand upon the page — a small page — where hers lay already. And when she pointed wrong, it was pleasant to correct her, over and over, insisting that her hand should be here, and not there, and lifting those little fingers from one page, and putting them down upon the other. And sometimes, half provoked with my fault-finding, she would pat my hand smartly with hers; but when I looked in her face to know what *that* could mean, she would meet my eye with such a kind submission and half earnest regret, as made me not only pardon the offence, but tempt me to provoke it again.

Through all the days of Carnival, when I rode pelted with *confetti*, and pelting back, my eyes used to wander up, from a long way off, to that tall house upon the Corso, where I was sure to meet, again and again, those forgiving eyes, and that soft brown hair, all gathered under the little brown *sombrero*, set off with one pure white plume. And her hand full of *bonbons* she would shake at me threateningly, and laugh — a musical laugh — as I bowed my head to the assault, and recovering from the shower of missiles, would turn to throw my stoutest bouquet at her balcony. At night I would bear home to the Roman parlor my best trophy of the day, as a guerdon for Enrica; and Enrica would be sure to render in acknowledgment some carefully hidden flowers, the prettiest that her beauty had won.

Sometimes upon those Carnival nights she arrays herself in the costume of the Albanian water-carriers; and nothing, one would think, could be prettier than the laced crimson jacket, and the strange head-gear with its trinkets, and the short skirts leaving to view as delicate an ankle as could be found in Rome. Upon another night she glides into my little parlor, as we sit by the blaze, in a close velvet bodice, and with a Swiss hat caught up by a looplet of silver, and adorned with a full-blown rose, — nothing you think could be prettier than this. Again, in one of her girlish freaks she robes herself like a nun; and with the heavy black serge for dress, and the funereal veil, — relieved only by the plain white ruffle of her cap, — you wish she were always a nun. But the wish vanishes when you see her in a pure white muslin, with a wreath of orange-blossoms about her forehead, and a single white rose-bud in her bosom.

Upon the little balcony Enrica keeps a pot or two of flowers, which bloom all winter long; and each morning I find upon my table a fresh rose-bud; each night I bear back for thank-offering the prettiest bouquet that can be found in the Via Condotti. The quiet fireside evenings come back, — in which my hand seeks its wonted place upon her book; and my other *will* creep around upon the back of Enrica's chair, and Enrica *will* look indignant — and then all forgiveness.

One day I received a large packet of letters. Ah, what luxury to lie back in my big arm-chair, there before the crackling fagots, with the pleasant rustle of that silken dress beside me, and run over a second and a third time those mute paper missives, which bore to me over so many miles of water the words of greeting and of love! It would be worth travelling to the shores of the Ægean, to find one's heart quickened into such life as the ocean letters will make. Enrica threw down her book, and wondered what could be in them? — and snatched one from my hand, and looked with sad but vain intensity over that strange scrawl. "What can it be?" said she; and she laid her finger upon the little half line — "Dear Paul."

I told her it was — "*Caro mio.*"

Enrica laid it upon her lap and looked in my face "It is from your mother?" said she.

"No," said I.

"From your sister?" said she.

"Alas, no!"

"*Il vostro fratello, dunque?*"

"*Nemmeno*," said I, "not from a brother either."

She handed me the letter, and took up her book and presently she laid the book down again, and looked at the letter, and then at me, — and went out.

She did not come in again that evening; in the morning there was no rose-bud on my table. And when I came at night, with a bouquet from Pietro's at the corner, she asked me who had written my letter.

" A very dear friend," said I.

" A lady ? " continued she.

" A lady," said I.

" Keep this bouquet for her," said she, and put it in my hands.

" But, Enrica, she has plenty of flowers: she lives among them, and each morning her children gather them by scores to make garlands of."

Enrica put her fingers within my hand to take again the bouquet; and for a moment I held both fingers and flowers.

The flowers slipped out first.

I had a friend at Rome in that time, who afterward died between Ancona and Corinth. We were sitting one day upon a block of tufa in the middle of the Coliseum, looking up at the shadows which the waving shrubs upon the southern wall cast upon the ruined arcades within, and listening to the chirping sparrows that lived upon the wreck, when he said to me suddenly, — " Paul, you love the Italian girl."

" She is very beautiful," said I.

" I think she is beginning to love you," said he, soberly.

"She has a very warm heart, I believe," said I.

"Aye," said he.

"But her feelings are those of a girl," continued I.

"They are not," said my friend; and he laid his hand upon my knee, and left off drawing diagrams with his cane. "I have seen, Paul, more than you of this southern nature. The Italian girl of fifteen is a woman, — an impassioned, sensitive, tender creature, — yet still a woman; you are loving — if you love — a full-grown heart; she is loving — if she loves — as a ripe heart should."

"But I do not think that either is wholly true," said I.

"Try it," said he, setting his cane down firmly, and looking in my face.

"How?" returned I.

"I have three weeks upon my hands," continued he. "Go with me into the Apennines; leave your home in the Corso, and see if you can forget in the air of the mountains your bright-eyed Roman girl!"

I was pondering for an answer, when he went on, — "It is better so: love as you might, that southern nature with all its passion is not the material to build domestic happiness upon; nor is your northern habit — whatever you may think at your time of life — the one to cherish always those passionate sympathies which are bred by this atmosphere and their scenes."

One moment my thought ran to my little parlor, and to that fairy figure, and to that sweet angel-face ; and then like lightning it traversed oceans, and fed upon the old ideal of home, and brought images to my eye of lost — dead ones, who seemed to be stirring on heavenly wings, in that soft Roman atmosphere, with greeting and with beckoning.

——" I will go with you," said I.

The father shrugged his shoulders when I told him I was going to the mountains and wanted a guide. His wife said it would be cold upon the hills, for the winter was not ended. Enrica said it would be warm in the valleys, for the spring was coming. The old man drummed with his fingers on the table, and shrugged his shoulders again, but said nothing.

My landlady said I could not ride. Cesare said it would be hard walking. Enrica asked papa if there would be any danger? And again the old man shrugged his shoulders. Again I asked him if he knew a man who would serve us as guide among the Apennines; and finding me determined, he shrugged his shoulders, and said he would find one the next day.

As I passed out at evening on my way to the Piazzo near the Monte Citorio, where stand the carriages that go out to Tivoli, Enrica glided up to me and whispered, "*Ah, mi dispiace tanto — tanto, Signor!*"

The Apennines.

I SHOOK her hand, and in an hour afterward was passing with my friend by the Trajan forum, toward the deep shadow of San Maggiore, which lay in our way to the mountains. At sunset we were wandering over the ruin of Adrian's villa, which lies upon the first step of the Apennines. Behind us, the vesper-bells of Tivoli were sounding, and their echoes floating sweetly under the broken arches; before us, stretching all the way to the horizon, lay the broad Campagna; while in the middle of its great waves, turned violet-colored by the hues of twilight, rose the grouped towers of the Eternal City; and lording it among them all, like a giant, stood the black dome of St. Peter's.

Day after day we stretched on over the mountains, leaving the Campagna far behind us. Rocks and stones, huge and ragged, lie strewed over the surface right and left; deep yawning valleys lie in the shadows of mountains that loom up thousands of feet, bearing perhaps upon their tops old castellated towns perched like birds'-nests. But mountain and valley are blasted and scarred; the forests even are not continuous, but struggle for a livelihood; as if the brimstone fire that consumed Nineveh had withered their energies. Some times our eyes rest on a great white scar of the broken calcareous rock, on which the moss cannot grow, and the lizards dare not creep. Then we see a cliff beetling far aloft, with the shining walls of some monastery of holy men glistening at its base. The wayside brooks do not seem to be the gentle offspring of bountiful hills, but the remnants of something greater whose greatness has expired;—they are turbid rills, rolling in the bottom of yawning chasms. Even the shrubs have a look as if the Volscian war-horse had trampled them down to death; and the primroses and the violets by the mountain-path alone look modestly beautiful amid the ruin.

Sometimes we loiter in a valley, above which the goats are browsing on the cliffs, and listen to the sweet pastoral pipes of the Apennines. We see the shepherds in their rough skin-coats high over our heads. Their herds are feeding, as it seems, on ledges of a hand's-breadth. The sweet sound floats and lingers in the soft atmosphere, without a breath of wind to bear it away, or a noise to disturb its melody. The shadows slant more and more as we linger; and the kids begin to group together. And as we wander on through the stunted vineyards in the bottom of the valley, the sweet sound flows after us like a river of song,—nor leaves us till the kids have vanished in the distance, and the cliffs themselves become one dark wall of shadow.

At night, in some little meagre mountain town, we stroll about in the narrow pass-ways, or wander under the heavy arches of the mountain churches. Shuf fling old women grope in and out; dim lamps glimmer faintly at the side-altars, shedding horrid light upon painted images of the dying Christ. Or perhaps, to make the old pile more solemn, there stands some bier in the middle, with a figure or two kneeling at the foot, and ragged boys move stealthily under the shadows of the columns. Presently comes a young priest in black robes, and lights a taper at the foot, and another at the head, — for there is a dead man on the bier; and the parched thin features look awfully under the yellow light of the tapers, in the gloom of the great building It is very, very damp in the church, and the body of the dead man seems to make the air heavy, so we go out into the starlight again.

In the morning, the western slopes wear broad shadows, and the frosts crumple on the herbage to our tread. Across the valley it is like summer; and the birds — for there are songsters in the Apennines — make summer music. Their notes blend softly with the faint sounds of some far-off convent-bell tolling for morning mass, and strike the frosted and shaded mountain-side with a sweet echo. As we toil on, and the shaded hills begin to glow in the sunshine, we pass a train of mules loaded with wine. We have seen them an hour before, — little black dots twining along the white streak of footway upon the mountain above us. We lost them as we began to ascend, until a wild snatch of an Apennine song turned our eyes up, and there, straggling through the brush, they appeared again; a foot-slip would have brought the mules and wine-casks rolling upon us. We keep still, holding by the brush wood, to let them pass. An hour more and we see them toiling slowly, — mule and muleteer, — big dots and little dots, — far down where we have been before. The sun is hot and smoking on them in the bare valleys; the sun is hot and smoking on the hillside, where we are toiling over the broken stones. I thought of little Enrica, when she said — the spring was coming!

Time and again, we sit down together — my friend and I — upon some fragment of rock, under the broad-armed chestnuts that fringe the lower skirts of the mountains, and talk through the hottest of the noon, of the warriors of Sylla, and of the Sabine women, — but oftener of the pretty peasantry, and of the sweet-faced Roman girl. He too tells me of his life and loves, and of the hopes that lie misty and grand before him: — little did we think that in so few years his hopes would be gone, and his body lying low in the Adriatic, or tost with the drift upon the Dalmatian shores! Little did I think that here under the ancestral wood — still a wishful and blundering mortal — I should be gathering up the shreds that memory can catch of our Apennine wandering, and be weaving them into my bachelor dreams.

Away again upon the quick wing of thought, I follow our steps, as, after weeks of wandering, we gained once more a height that overlooked the Campagna, and saw the sun setting on its edge, throwing into relief the dome of St. Peter's, and blazing in a red stripe upon the waters of the Tiber.

Below us was Palestrina, — the Præneste of the poets and philosophers, — the dwelling-place of — I know not how many — Emperors. We went straggling through the dirty streets, searching for some tidy-looking *osteria*. At length we found an old lady, who could give us a bed, but no dinner. My friend dropped in a chair disheartened. A snub-looking priest came out to condole with us.

And could Palestrina, — the *frigidum Præneste* of Horace, which had entertained over and over the noblest of the Colonna, and the most noble Adrian, — could Palestrina not furnish a dinner to a tired traveller?

" *Si, Signore,*" said the snub-looking priest.

" *Si, Signorino,*" said the neat old lady; and away we went upon a new search. And we found bright and happy faces, — especially the little girl of twelve years, who came close by me as I ate, and afterward strung a garland of marigolds, and put it on my head. Then there was a bright-eyed boy of fourteen, who wrote his name and those of the whole family upon a fly-leaf of my book; and a pretty, saucy-looking girl of sixteen, who peeped a long time from behind the kitchen-door, but before the evening was gone she was in the chair beside me, and had written her name — Carlotta — upon the first leaf of my journal.

When I woke, the sun was up. From my bed I could see over the town the thin, lazy mists lying on the old camp-ground of Pyrrhus; beyond it were the mountains which hide Frascati, and Monte-Cavi. There was old Colonna, too, that,

> " Like an eagle's nest hangs on the crest
> Of purple Apennine " *

As the mist lifted and the sun brightened the plain, I could see the road along which Sylla came fuming and maddened after the Mithridatic war. I could see, as I half-dreamed and half-slept, the frightened peasantry whooping to their long-horned cattle, as they drove them on tumultuously up through the gateways of the town; and women with babies in their arms, and children scowling with fear and hate, — all trooping fast and madly to escape the hand of the Avenger; alas ineffectually, for Sylla murdered them, and pulled down the walls of their town — the proud Palestrina!

I had a queer fancy of seeing the nobles of Rome, led on by Stefano Colonna, grouping along the plain, their

* Macaulay's *Horatius*.

corselet sflashing out of the mists, their pennons dashing above it, coming up fast and still as the wind, to make the Mural Præneste their stronghold against the Last of the Tribunes. And strangely mingling fiction with fact, I saw the brother of Walter de Montreal, with his noisy and bristling army, crowd over the Campagna, and put up his white tents, and hang out his showy banners, on the grassy knolls that lay nearest my eye.

—— But the knolls were all quiet; there was not so much as a strolling *contadino* on them to whistle a mimic fife-note. A little boy from the inn went with me upon the hill, to look out upon the town and the wide sea of land below; and whether it was the soft, warm April sun, or the gray ruins below me, or whether the wonderful silence of the scene, or some wild gush of memory, I do not know, but something made me sad.

"*Perché cosi penseroso?* — Why so sad?" said the quick-eyed boy. "The air is beautiful, the scene is beautiful; Signore is young, — why is he sad?"

"And is Giovanni never sad?" said I.

"*Quasi mai*," said the boy; "and if I could travel as Signore, and see other countries, I would be always gay."

"May you be always that!" said I.

The good wish touched him; he took me by the arms and said, "Go home with me, Signore; you were happy at the inn last night; go back, and we will make you gay again!"

—— If we could be always boys!

I thanked him in a way that saddened him. We passed out shortly after from the city gates, and strode on over the rolling plain. Once or twice we turned back to look at the rocky heights beneath which lay the ruined town of Palestrina, — a city that defied Rome, that had a king before a ploughshare had touched the Capitoline, or the Janiculan hill! The ivy was covering up richly the Etruscan foundations, and there was a quiet over the whole place. The smoke was rising straight into the sky from the chimney-tops; a peasant or two were going along the road with donkeys; beside this, the city was to all appearance a dead city. And it seemed to me that an old monk, whom I could see with my glass near the little chapel above the town, might be going to say mass for the soul of the dead city.

And afterward, when we came near to Rome, and passed under the temple-tomb of Metella, my friend said, "And will you go back now to your home? or will you set off with me to-morrow for Ancona?"

"At least I must say adieu," returned I.

"God speed you!" said he; and we parted upon the Piazza di Venezia, — he for his last mass at St. Peter's, and I for the tall house upon the Corso.

Enrica.

I HEAR her glancing feet the moment I have tinkled the bell; and there she is, with her brown hair gathered into braids, and her eyes full of joy and greeting. And as I walk with the mother to the window, to look at some pageant that is passing, she steals up behind, and passes her arm around me with a quick, electric motion, and a gentle pressure of welcome, that tells more than a thousand words.

It is a pageant of death that is passing below. Far down the street we see heads thrust out of the windows, and standing in bold relief against the red torch-light of the moving train. Below, dim figures are gathering on the narrow side-ways to look at the solemn spectacle. A hoarse chant rises louder and louder, and half dies in the night-air, and breaks out again with new and deep bitterness.

Now the first torch-light under us shines plainly on faces in the windows, and on the kneeling women in the street. First come old retainers of the dead one, bearing long, blazing flambeaux. Then comes a company of priests, two by two, bareheaded, and every second one with a lighted torch, and all are chanting.

Next is a brotherhood of friars in brown cloaks, with sandalled feet; and the red light streams full upon their grizzled heads. They add their heavy guttural voices to the chant, and pass slowly on.

Then comes a company of priests, in white muslin capes, and black robes, and black caps, bearing books in their hands wide open, and lit up plainly by the torches of churchly servitors who march beside them; and from the books the priests chant loud and solemnly Now the music is loudest; and the friars take up the dismal notes from the white-caped priests, and the priests before catch them from the brown-robed friars, and mournfully the sound rises up between the tall buildings into the blue night-sky that lies between heaven and Rome.

— "*Vede, vede!*" says Cesare; and in a blaze of the red torch-fire comes the bier, borne on the necks of stout friars; and on the bier is the body of a dead man habited like a priest. Heavy plumes of black wave at each corner.

— "Hist!" says my landlady.

The body is just under us. Enrica crosses herself; her smile is for the moment gone. Cesare's boy-face is grown suddenly earnest. We could see the pale, youthful features of the dead man. The glaring flambeaux sent their flaunting streams of unearthly light over the wan visage of the sleeper. A thousand eyes were looking on him; but his face, careless of them all, was turned up straight toward the stars.

Still the chant rises; and companies of priests follow the bier like those who had gone before. Friars in brown cloaks, and prelates and Carmelites, come after all with torches. Two by two — their voices growing hoarse — they tramp, and chant.

For a while the voices cease, and you can hear the rustling of their robes, and their footfalls, as if your ear was to the earth. Then the chant rises again as they glide on in a wavy, shining line, and rolls back over the death-train, like the howling of a wind in winter.

As they pass, the faces vanish from the windows. The kneeling women upon the pavement rise up, mindful of the paroxysm of Life once more. The groups in the doorways scatter. But their low voices do not drown the voices of the host of mourners and their ghost-like music.

I look long upon the blazing bier trailing under the deep shadows of the Roman palaces, and at the stream of torches winding like a glittering, scaled serpent. — "It is a priest," say I to my landlady, as she closes the window.

" No, signor, — a young man never married; and so by virtue of his condition they put on him the priest-robes."

" So I," says the pretty Enrica, " if I should die, would be robed in white, as you saw me on a Carnival night, and be followed by nuns for sisters."

" A long way off may it be, Enrica ! "

She took my hand in hers and pressed it. An Italian

girl does not fear to talk of death; and we were talking of it still as we walked back to my little parlor — my hand all the time in hers — and sat down by the blaze of my fire.

It was Holy Week. Never had Enrica looked more sweetly than in that black dress, — under that long, dark veil of the days of Lent. Upon the broad pavement of St. Peter's, where the people, flocking by thousands, made only side-groups about the altars of the vast temple, I have watched her kneeling beside her mother, her eyes bent down, her lips moving earnestly, and her whole figure tremulous with deep emotion. Wandering around among the halberdiers of the Pope, and the court-coats of Austria, and the barefooted pilgrims with sandal, shell, and staff, I would sidle back again, to look upon that kneeling figure; and leaning against the huge columns of the church, would dream — even as I am dreaming now.

At nightfall I urge my way into the Sistine Chapel. Enrica is beside me, looking with me upon the gaunt figures of the Judgment of Angelo. They are chanting the *Miserere*. The twelve candlesticks by the altar are put out one by one, as the service continues. The sun has gone down, and only the red glow of twilight steals through the dusky windows. There is a pause, and a brief reading from a red-cloaked cardinal, and all kneel down. *She* kneels beside me; and the sweet mournful flow of the *Miserere* begins again, growing in force and depth till the whole chapel rings, and the balcony of the choir trembles; then it subsides again into the low, soft wail of a single voice, so prolonged, so tremulous, and so real, that the heart aches, and the ears start — for Christ is dead!

—— Lingering yet, the wail dies not wholly, but, just as it seemed expiring, it is caught up by another and stronger voice that carries it on, plaintive as ever; — nor does it stop with this; for just as you looked for silence, three voices more begin the lament, — sweet, touching, mournful voices, — and bear it up to a full cry, when the whole choir catch its burden, and make the lament change into the wailing of a multitude, — wild, shrill, hoarse, — with swift chants intervening, as if agony had given force to anguish. Then, sweetly, slowly, voice by voice, note by note, the wailings sink into the low, tender moan of a single singer — faltering, tremulous, as if tears checked the utterance, and swelling out as if despair sustained it.

It was dark in the chapel when we went out; voices were low. Enrica said nothing, — I could say nothing.

I was to leave Rome after Easter. I did not love to speak of it, nor to think of it. Rome — that old city, with all its misery, and its fallen state, and its broken palaces of the Empire — grows upon one's heart. The fringing shrubs of the Coliseum, flaunting their blossoms at the tall beggarmen in cloaks, who grub below, — the sun glimmering over the mossy pile of the House of Nero, — the sweet sunsets from the Pincian, that make the broad pine-tops of the Janiculan stand sharp and dark against a sky of gold, — cannot easily be left behind. And Enrica, with her silver-brown hair, and the silken fillet that bound it, — and her deep hazel eyes, — and her white, delicate fingers, — and the blue veins chasing over her fair temples, — ah, Easter is too near!

But it comes; and passes with the glory of St. Peter's — lighted from top to bottom. With Enrica, I saw it from the Ripetta, as it loomed up in the distance, like a city on fire.

The next day I bring home my last bunch of flowers, and with it a little richly chased Roman ring. No fire blazes on the hearth, — but they are all there. Warm days have come, and the summer air even now hangs heavy with fever, in the hollows of the plain.

I heard them stirring early on the morning on which I was to go away. I do not think I slept very well myself — nor very late. Never did Enrica look more beautiful — never. All her Carnival robes, and the sad drapery of the Friday of Crucifixion, could not so adorn her beauty as that neat morning-dress, and that simple rose-bud she wore upon her bosom. She gave it to me — the last — with a trembling hand. I did not, for I could not, thank her. She knew it; and her eyes were full.

The old man kissed my cheek, — it was the Roman custom, but the custom did not extend to the Roman girls, at least not often. As I passed down the Corso I looked back at the balcony, where she stood in the time of Carnival, in the brown *sombrero* with the white plume. I knew she would be there now; and there she was. My eyes dwelt upon the vision, very loth to leave it; and after my eyes had lost it, my heart clung to it, — there, where my memory clings now.

At noon, the carriage stopped upon the hills toward Soracte, that overlooked Rome. There was a stunted pine-tree grew a little way from the road, and I sat down under it, — for I wished no dinner, — and I looked back with strange tumult of feeling upon the sleeping city, with the gray, billowy sea of the Campagna lying around it.

I seemed to see Enrica — the Roman girl — in that morning-dress, with her brown hair in its silken fillet; but the rose-bud, that was in her bosom, was now in mine. Her silvery voice too seemed to float past me, bearing snatches of Roman songs; but the songs were sad and broken.

—— After all, this is sad vanity! thought I; and yet if I had espied then some returning carriage going down toward Rome, I will not say — but that I should have hailed it, and taken a place, and gone back, and to this day, perhaps — have lived at Rome.

But the *vetturino* called me; the coach was ready; I gave one more look toward the dome that guarded the sleeping city; and then we galloped down the mountain on the road that lay towards Perugia and Lake Thrasimene.

—— Sweet Enrica! art thou living yet? Or hast thou passed away to that Silent Land where the good sleep and the beautiful?

The visions of the Past fade. The morning breeze has died upon the meadow; the Bob-o'-Lincoln sits swaying upon the willow-turfs, singing no longer. The trees lean to the brook; but the shadows fall straight and dense upon the silver stream.

Noon has broken into the middle sky; and Morning is gone.

II.

Noon.

THE Noon is short; the sun never loiters on the meridian, nor does the shadow on the old dial by the garden stay long at XII. The Present, like the noon, is only a point, and a point so fine, that it is not measurable by the grossness of action. Thought alone is delicate enough to tell the breadth of the Present.

The Past belongs to God; the Present only is ours. And short as it is, there is more in it and of it than we can well manage. That man who can grapple it, and measure it, and fill it with his purpose, is doing a man's work; none can do more; but there are thousands who do less.

Short as it is, the Present is great and strong, — as much stronger than the Past as fire than ashes, or as Death than the grave. The noon sun will quicken vegetable life that in the morning was dead. It is hot and scorching; I feel it now upon my head; but it does not scorch and heat like the bewildering Present. There are no oak-leaves to interrupt the rays of the burning Now. Its shadows do not fall east or west·

like the noon, the shade it makes falls straight from sky to earth,—straight from Heaven to Hell!

Memory presides over the Past; Action presides over the Present. The first lives in a rich temple hung with glorious trophies and lined with tombs; the other has no shrine but Duty, and it walks the earth like a spirit!

—— I called my dog to me, and we shared together the meal that I had brought away at sunrise from the mansion under the elms; and now Carlo is gnawing at the bone that I have thrown to him, and I stroll dreamily in the quiet noon atmosphere upon that grassy knoll under the oaks.

Noon in the country is very still: the birds do not sing; the workmen are not in the field; the sheep lay their noses to the ground; and the herds stand in pools under shady trees, lashing their sides, but otherwise motionless. The mills upon the brook far above have ceased for an hour their labor; and the stream softens its rustle, and sinks away from the sedgy banks. The heat plays upon the meadow in noiseless waves, and the beech-leaves do not stir.

Thought, I said, was the only measure of the Present; and the stillness of noon breeds thought, and my thought brings up the old companions, and stations them in the domain of Now. Thought ranges over the world, and brings up hopes and fears and resolves to measure the burning Now. Joy, and grief, and purpose, blending in my thought, give breadth to the Present.

— Where, thought I, is little Isabel now? Where is Lilly; where is Ben? Where is Leslie; where is my old teacher? Where is my chum who played such rare tricks? Where is the black-eyed Jane? Where is that sweet-faced girl whom I parted with upon that terrace looking down upon the old spire of Madbury church? Where are my hopes; where my purposes; where my sorrows?

I care not who you are, but if you bring such thought to measure the Present, the Present will seem broad; and it will be sultry as noon, and make a fever of Now.

Early Friends.

Where are they?

I cannot sit now, as once, upon the edge of the brook, hour after hour, flinging off my line and hook to the nibbling roach, and reckon it great sport. There is no girl with auburn ringlets to sit beside me, and to play upon the bank. The hours are shorter than they were then; and the little joys that furnished boyhood till the heart was full, can fill it no longer. Poor Tray is dead long ago, and he cannot swim into the pools for the floating sticks; nor can I sport with him hour after hour, and think it happiness. The mound that covers his grave is sunken, and the trees that shaded it are broken and mossy.

Little Lilly is grown into a woman, and is married; and she has another little Lilly, with flaxen hair, she says, — looking as *she* used to look. I dare say the child is pretty; but it is not my Lilly. She has a little boy, too, that she calls Paul, — a chubby rogue, she writes, and as mischievous as ever I was. God bless the boy!

Ben, who would have liked to ride in the coach that carried me away to school, has had a great many rides since then, — rough rides, and hard ones, over the road of life. He does not rake up the falling leaves for bonfires, as he did once; he is grown a man, and is fighting his way somewhere in our western world to the short-lived honors of time. He was married not long ago; his wife I remembered as one of my playmates at my first school; she was beautiful, but fragile as a leaf. She died within a year of their marriage. Ben was but four years my senior, but this grief has made him ten years older. He does not say it, but his eye and his figure tell it.

The nurse, who put the purse in my hand that dismal morning, is grown a feeble old woman. She was over fifty then; she may well be seventy now. She did not know my voice when I went to see her the other day, nor did she know my face at all. She repeated the name when I told it to her: Paul, Paul,—she did not remember any Paul except a little boy, a long while ago.

——" To whom you gave a purse when he went away, and told him to say nothing to Lilly or to Ben?"

"Yes; that Paul," says the old woman, exultingly do you know him?"

And when I told her,—" she would not have believed it!" But she did, and took hold of my hand again (for she was blind); and then smoothed down the plaits of her apron, and jogged her cap-strings, to look tidy in the presence of "the gentleman." And she told me long stories about the old house, and how other people came in afterward; and she called me "sir" sometimes, and sometimes "Paul." But I asked her to say only Paul; she seemed glad for this, and talked easier; and went on to tell of my old playmates, and how we used to ride the pony,—poor Jacko!—and how we gathered nuts,—such heaping piles; and how we used to play at fox-and-geese through the long winter evenings; and how my poor mother would smile——but here I asked her to stop. She could not have gone on much longer, for I believe she loved our house and people better than she loved her own.

As for my uncle, the cold, silent man, who lived with his books in the house upon the hill, and who used to frighten me sometimes with his look, he grew very feeble after I had left, and almost crazed. The country-people said that he was mad; and Isabel with her sweet heart clung to him, and would lead him out, when his step tottered, to the seat in the garden, and read to him out of the books he loved to hear. And sometimes, they told me, she would read to him some letters that I had written to Lilly or to Ben, and ask him if he remembered Paul, who saved her from drowning under the tree in the meadow? But he could only shake his head, and mutter something about how old and feeble he had grown.

They wrote me afterward that he died; and was buried in a far-away place, where his wife once lived, and where he now sleeps beside her. Isabel was sick with grief, and came to live for a time with Lilly; but when they wrote me last, she had gone back to her old home, — where Tray was buried, — where we had played together so often through the long days of summer.

I was glad I should find her there when I came back Lilly and Ben were both living nearer to the city when I landed from my long journey over the seas; but still I went to find Isabel first. Perhaps I had heard so much oftener from the others that I felt less eager to see them; or perhaps I wanted to save my best visits to the last; or perhaps (I did think it) — perhaps I loved Isabel better than them all.

So I went into the country, thinking all the way how she must have changed since I left. She must be now nineteen or twenty; and then her grief must have saddened her face somewhat; but I thought I should like her all the better for that. Then perhaps she would not laugh, and tease me, but would be quieter, and wear a sweet smile, — so calm and beautiful, I thought. Her figure too must have grown more elegant, and she would have more dignity in her air.

I shuddered a little at this; for I thought, — she will hardly think so much of me then; perhaps she will have seen those whom she likes a great deal better Perhaps she will not like me at all; yet I knew very well that I should like her.

I had gone up almost to the house; I had passed the stream where we fished on that day, many years before; and I thought that now since she was grown to womanhood, I should never sit with her there again, and surely never drag her as I did out of the water, and never chafe her little hands, and never perhaps kiss her as I did when she sat upon my mother's lap, — oh, no — no — no!

I saw where we buried Tray, but the old slab was gone; there was no ribbon there now. I thought that at least Isabel would have replaced the slab; but it was a wrong thought. I trembled when I went up to the door; for it flashed upon me, that perhaps Isabel was married. I could not tell why she should not; but I knew it would make me uncomfortable to hear that she had.

There was a tall woman, who opened the door; she did not know me; but I recognized her as one of the old servants. I asked after the housekeeper first, thinking I would surprise Isabel. My heart fluttered somewhat, thinking that she might step in suddenly herself, or perhaps that she might have seen me coming up the hill. But even then, I thought, she would hardly know me.

Presently the housekeeper came in, looking very grave; she asked if the gentleman wished to see her?

The gentleman did wish it, and she sat down on one side of the fire; for it was autumn, and the leaves were falling, and the November winds were very chilly.

—— Shall I tell her, thought I, who I am, or ask at once for Isabel? I tried to ask; but it was hard for me to call her name; it was very strange, but I could not pronounce it at all.

"Who, sir?" said the housekeeper, in a tone so earnest that I rose at once, and crossed over, and took her hand: "You know me," said I, — "you surely remember Paul?"

She started with surprise, but recovered herself and resumed the same grave manner. I thought I had committed some mistake, or been in some way cause of offence. I called her "madam," and asked for—Isabel.

"She turned pale, terribly pale; "Bella?" said she.

"Yes, Bella."

"Sir, Bella is dead!"

I dropped into my chair. I said nothing. The housekeeper—bless her kind heart!—slipped noiselessly out. My hands were over my eyes. The winds were sighing outside, and the clock ticking mournfully within.

I did not sob, nor weep, nor utter any cry.

The clock ticked mournfully, and the winds were sighing; but I did not hear them any longer; there was a tempest raging within me, that would have drowned the voice of thunder.

It broke at length in a long, deep sigh: "O God!" said I. It may have been a prayer; it was not an imprecation.

Bella—sweet Bella was dead! It seemed as if with her half the world were dead,—every bright face darkened,—every sunshine blotted out,—every flower withered,—every hope extinguished!

I walked out into the air and stood under the trees where we had played together with poor Tray,—where Tray lay buried. But it was not Tray I thought of, as I stood there, with the cold wind playing through my hair, and my eyes filling with tears. How could she lie? Why *was* she gone? Was it really true? Was Isabel indeed dead, — in her coffin, — buried? Then why should anybody live? What was there to live for now that Bella was gone?

Ah, what a gap in the world is made by the death of those we love! It is no longer whole, but a poor half-world, that swings uneasy on its axis, and makes you dizzy with the clatter of its wreck!

The housekeeper told me all, little by little, as I found calmness to listen. She had been dead a month Lilly was with her through it all; she died sweetly, without pain, and without fear, — what can angels fear? She had spoken often of " Cousin Paul "; she had left a little packet for him, but it was not there; she had given it into Lilly's keeping.

Her grave, the housekeeper told me, was only a little way off from her home, — beside the grave of a brother who died long years before. I went there that evening. The mound was high and fresh. The sods had not closed together, and the dry leaves caught in the crevices, and gave a ragged and a terrible look to the grave. The next day I laid them all smooth, — as we had once laid them on the grave of Tray; I clipped the long grass, and set a tuft of blue violets at the foot, and watered it all with — tears. The homestead, the trees, the fields, the meadows, in the windy November, looked dismally. I could not like them again; I liked nothing— but the little mound I had dressed over Bella's grave. There she sleeps now,— the sleep of Death!

School Revisited.

THE old school is there still, with the high cupola upon it, and the long galleries, with the sleeping-rooms opening out on either side, and the corner one where I slept. But the boys are not there, nor the old teachers. They have ploughed up the play-ground to plant corn; and the apple-tree with the low limb, that made our gymnasium, is cut down.

I was there only a little time ago. It was on Sunday. One of the old houses of the village had been fashioned into a tavern, and it was there I stopped. But I strolled by the old one, and looked into the bar-room, where I used to gaze with wonder upon the enormous pictures of wild animals, which heralded some coming menagerie. There was just such a picture hanging still, and two or three advertisements of sheriffs, and a little bill of a "horse stolen," and, as I thought, the same brown pitcher on the edge of the bar. I was sure it was the same great wood-box that stood by the fireplace, and the same whip and great-coat hung in the corner.

I was not in so gay a costume as I once thought I would be wearing, when a man; I had nothing better than a rusty shooting-jacket; but even with this I was determined to have a look about the church, and see if I could trace any of the faces of the old times. They had sadly altered the building; they had cut out its long galleries, and its old-fashioned square pews, and filled it with narrow boxes, as they do in the city. The pulpit was not so high, or grand; and it was covered over with the work of the cabinet-makers.

I missed, too, the old preacher whom we all feared so much; and in place of him was a jaunty-looking man, whom I thought I would not be at all afraid to speak to, or, if need be, to slap on the shoulder. And when I did meet him after church, I looked him in the eye as boldly as a lion;—what a change was that from the school-days!

Here and there I could detect about the church some old farmer, by the stoop in his shoulders, or by a particular twist in his nose; and one or two young fellows, who used to storm into the gallery in my school-days, in very gay jackets dressed off with ribbons,—which we thought was astonishing heroism, and admired accordingly,—were now settled away into fathers of families and looked as demure and peaceable at the head of their pews, with a white-headed boy or two between them and their wives, as if they had been married all their days.

There was a stout man, too, with a slight limp in his

gait, who used to work on harnesses, and strap our skates, and who I always thought would have made a capital Vulcan; he stalked up the aisle past me as if I had my skates strapped at his shop only yesterday.

The bald-pated shoemaker, who never kept his word, and who worked in the brick shop, and who had a son called Theodore, — which we all thought a very pretty name for a shoemaker's son, — I could not find. I feared he might be dead. I hoped, if he was, that his broken promises about patching boots would not come up against him.

The old factor of tamarinds and sugar-crackers, who used to drive his covered wagon every Saturday evening into the play-ground, I observed, still holding his place in the village choir, and singing — though with a tooth or two gone — as serenely and obstreporously as ever.

I looked around the church to find the black-eyed girl, who always sat behind the choir, — the one I loved to look at so much. I knew she must be grown up; but I could fix upon no face positively; once, as a stout woman with a pair of boys, and who wore a big red shawl, turned half-round, I thought I recognized her nose. If it was she, it had grown red though, and I felt cured of my old fondness. As for the other, who wore the hat trimmed with fur, she was nowhere to be seen, among either maids or matrons; and when I asked the tavern-keeper, and described her and her father as they were in my school-days, he told me that she had married too, and lived some five miles from the village; and, said he, "I guess she leads her husband a devil of a life!"

I felt cured of her too; but I pitied the husband.

One of my old teachers was in the church; I could have sworn to his face; he was a precise man, and now I thought he looked rather roughly at my old shooting-jacket. But I let him look, and scowled at him a little; for I remembered that he had feruled me once. I thought it was not probable that he would ever do it again.

There was a bustling little lawyer in the village, who lived in a large house, and who was the great man of that town and country: he had scarce changed at all; and he stepped into the church as briskly and promptly as he did ten years ago. But what struck me most was the change in a couple of pretty little white-haired girls that at the time I left were of that uncertain age when the mother lifts them on a Sunday, and pounces them down one after the other upon the seat of the pew;— these were now grown into blooming young ladies. And they swept by me in the vestibule of the church, with a flutter of robes and a grace of motion that fairly made my heart twitter in my bosom. I know nothing that brings home upon a man so quick the consciousness of increasing years, as to find the little prattling girls, that were almost babies in his boyhood, become dashing ladies; and to find those whom he used to look on patronizingly and compassionately — thinking they were little girls — grown to such maturity that the mere rustle of their silk dress will give him a twinge, and their eyes, if he looks at them, make him unaccountably shy.

After service I strolled up by the school-buildings; I traced the names that we had cut upon the fence; but the fence had grown brown with age, and was nearly rotted away. Upon the beech-tree in the hollow behind the school, the carvings were all overgrown. It must have been vacation, if indeed there was any school at all; for I could see only one old woman about the premises, and she was hanging out a dishcloth to dry in the sun. I passed on up the hill, beyond the buildings where, in the boy-days, we built stone forts with bastions and turrets; but the farmers had put bastions and turrets into their cobble-stone walls. At the orchard-fence I stopped and looked — from force, I believe, of old habit — to see if any one were watching, and then leaped over, and found my way to the early apple-tree; but the fruit had gone by. It seemed very daring in me, even then, to walk so boldly in the forbidden ground.

But the old head-master, who forbade it, was dead,

and Russell and Burgess, and I know not how many others, who in other times were culprits with me, were dead too. When I passed back by the school, I lingered to look up at the windows of that corner-room where I had slept the sound, healthful sleep of boyhood and where, too, I had passed many, many wakeful hours, thinking of the absent Bella and of my home.

—— How small seem now the great griefs of boyhood! Light, floating clouds will obscure the sun that is but half risen; but let him be up mid-heaven, and the cloud that then darkens the land must be thick and heavy indeed.

—— The tears started from my eyes; was not such a cloud over me now?

College.

SCHOOLMATES slip out of sight and knowledge, and are forgotten; or if you meet them, they bear another character; the boy is not there. It is a new acquaintance that you make, with nothing of your fellow upon the benches but the name. Though the eye and face cleave to your memory, and you meet them afterward and think you have met a friend, the voice or the action will break down the charm, and you find only — another man.

But with your classmates in that later school, where

form and character were both nearer ripeness, and where knowledge, labored for together, bred the first manly sympathies, it is different. And as you meet them or hear of them, the thought of their advance makes a measure of your own, — it makes a measure of the Now.

You judge of your happiness by theirs; of your progress by theirs; and of your prospects by theirs. If one is happy, you seek to trace out the way by which he has wrought his happiness; you consider how it differs from your own; and you think with sighs how you might possibly have wrought the same, but *now* it has escaped. If another has won some honorable distinction, you fall to thinking how the man — your old equal, as you thought, upon the college-benches — has outrun you. It pricks to effort, and teaches the difference between now and then. Life with all its duties and hopes gathers upon your Present like a great weight, or like a storm ready to burst. It is met anew; it pleads more strongly; and action, that has been neglected, rises before you, a giant of remorse.

Stop not, loiter not, look not backward, if you would be among the foremost! The great Now — so quick, so broad, so fleeting — is yours; in an hour it will belong to the Eternity of the Past. The temper of Life is to be made good by big, honest blows; stop striking, and you will do nothing; strike feebly, and you will do almost as little. Success rides on every hour; grapple it, and you may win; but without a grapple it will never go with you. Work is the weapon of honor, and who lacks the weapon will never triumph.

There were some seventy of us,— all scattered now. I meet one here and there at wide distances apart; and we talk together of old days, and of our present work and life,— and separate. Just so ships at sea, in murky weather, will shift their course to come within hailing distance, and compare their longtitude, and — part. One I have met wandering in Southern Italy dreaming as I was dreaming,— over the tomb of Virgil by the dark grotto of Posilippo. It seemed strange to talk of our old readings in Tacitus there upon classic ground; but we did; and ran on to talk of our lives; and sitting down upon the promontory of Baiæ, looking off upon that blue sea, as clear as the classics, we told each other our respective stories. And two nights after, upon the quay, in sight of Vesuvius, which shed a lurid glow upon the sky, that was reflected from the white walls of the Hotel de Russie, and from the broad 'ava pavements, we parted,— he to wander among the isles of the Ægean, and I to turn northward.

Another time, as I was wandering among those mysterious figures that crowd the *foyer* of the French opera upon a night of the masked ball, I saw a familiar face I followed it with my eye, until I became convinced

He did not know me, until I named his old seat upon the bench of the division-room, and the hard-faced Tutor G——. Then we talked of the old rivalries, and Christmas jollities, and of this and that one, whom we had come upon in our wayward tracks, while the black-robed grisettes stared through their velvet masks; nor did we tire of comparing the old memories with the unearthly gayety of the scene about us, until daylight broke.

In a quiet mountain town of New England I came not long since upon another: he was hale and hearty and pushing his lawyer work with just the same nervous energy with which he used to recite a theorem of Euclid. He was father, too, of a couple of stout, curly-pated boys; and his good woman, as he called her, appeared a sensible, honest, good-natured lady. I must say that I envied him his wife, much more than I had envied my companion of the opera — his domino.

I happened only a little while ago to drop into the college chapel of a Sunday. There were the same hard oak benches below, and the lucky fellows who enjoyed a corner seat were leaning back upon the rail, after the old fashion. The tutors were perched up in their side-boxes, looking as prim and serious and important as ever. The same stout Doctor read the hymn in the same rhythmical way; and he prayed the same prayer, for (I thought) the same old sort of sinners.

As I shut my eyes to listen, it seemed as if the intermediate years had all gone out; and that I was on my own pew-bench, and thinking out those little schemes for excuses, or for effort, which were to relieve me, or to advance me, in my college world.

There was a pleasure — like the pleasure of dreaming about forgotten joys — in listening to the Doctor's sermon: he began in the same half embarrassed, half awkward way; and fumbled at his Bible-leaves, and the poor pinched cushion, as he did long before. But as he went on with his rusty and polemic vigor, the poetry within him would now and then warm his soul into a burst of fervid eloquence, and his face would glow, and his hand tremble, and the cushion and the Bible-leaves be all forgot, in the glow of his thought, until with a half cough, and a pinch at the cushion, he fell back into his strong but tread-mill argumentation.

In the corner above was the stately, white-haired professor, wearing the old dignity of carriage, and a smile as bland as if the years had all been playthings; and had I seen him in his lecture-room, I dare say I should have found the same suavity of address, the same marvellous currency of talk, and the same infinite composure over the exploding retorts.

Near him was the silver-haired old gentleman, — with a very astute expression, — who used to have an odd habit of tightening his cloak about his nether limbs. I could not see that his eye was any the less bright; nor did he seem less eager to catch at the handle of some witticism, or bit of satire, — to the poor student's cost. I remembered my old awe of him, I must say, with something of a grudge; but I had got fairly over it now. There are sharper griefs in life than a professor's talk.

Farther on I saw the long-faced, dark-haired man, who looked as if he were always near some explosive electric battery, or upon an insulated stool. He was, I believe, a man of fine feelings; but he had a way of reducing all action to dry, hard, mathematical system, with very little poetry about it. I know there was not much poetry in his problems in physics, and still less in his half-yearly examinations. But I do not dread them now.

Over opposite, I was glad to see still the aged head of the kind and generous old man, who, in my day, presided over the college; and who carried with him the affections of each succeeding class, — added to their respect for his learning. This seems a higher triumph to me now than it seemed then. A strong mind, or a cultivated mind may challenge respect; but here is needed a noble one to win affection.

A new man now filled his place in the president's seat; but he was one whom I had known, and been proud to know. His figure was bent and thin, — the very figure that an old Flemish master would have chosen for a scholar. His eye had a kind of piercing lustre, as if it had long been fixed on books; and his expression — when unrelieved by his affable smile — was that of hard midnight toil. With all his polish of mind, he was a gentleman at heart, and treated us always with a manly courtesy that is not forgotten.

But of all the faces that used to be ranged below, — four hundred men and boys, — there was not one with whom to join hands, and live back again. Their griefs, joys, and toil were chaining them to their labor of life. Each one in his thought, coursing over a world as wide as my own, — how many thousand worlds of thought upon this one world of ours!

I stepped dreamily through the corridors of the old Athenæum, thinking of that first fearful step when the faces were new, and the stern tutor was strange, and the prolix Livy *so* hard. I went up at night and skulked around the buildings when the lights were blazing from all the windows, and they were busy with their tasks, — plain tasks, and easy tasks, because they are certain tasks. Happy fellows, thought I, who have only to do what is set before you to be done. But the time is coming, and very fast, when you must not only do, but know what to do. The time is coming when in place of your one master you will have a thousand masters, — masters of duty, of business, of pleasure, and of grief, — giving you harder lessons each one of them than any of your Fluxions.

Morning will pass, and the Noon will come — hot and scorching.

The Packet of Bella.

I HAVE not forgotten that packet of Beila; I did not once forget it. And when I saw Lilly, — now the grown-up Lilly, — happy in her household, and blithe as when she was a maiden, she gave it to me. She told me too of Bella's illness, and of her suffering, and of her manner, when she put the little packet in her hand "for Cousin Paul." But this I will not repeat, — I cannot.

I know not why it was, but I shuddered at the mention of her name. There are some who will talk at table, and in their gossip, of dead friends; I wonder how they do it? For myself, when the grave has closed its gates on the faces of those I love, however busy my mournful thought may be, the tongue is silent. I cannot name their names; it shocks me to hear them named. It seems like tearing open half-healed wounds, and disturbing with harsh, worldly noise the sweet sleep of death.

I loved Bella. I know not how I loved her, whether

as a lover, or as a husband loves a wife; I only know this, — I always loved her. She was so gentle, so beautiful, so confiding, that I never once thought but that the whole world loved her as well as I. There was only one thing I never told to Bella: I would tell her of all my grief, and of all my joys; I would tell her my hopes, my ambitious dreams, my disappointments, my anger, and my dislikes; but I never told her how much I loved her.

I do not know why, unless I knew that it was needless. But I should as soon have thought of telling Bella, on some winter's day, " Bella, it is winter!"— or of whispering to her on some balmy day of August, " Bella, it is summer!"— as of telling her, after she had grown to girlhood, " Bella, I love you!"

I had received one letter from her in the old countries; it was a sweet letter, in which she told me all that she had been doing, and how she had thought of me when she rambled over the woods where we had rambled together. She had written two or three other letters, Lilly told me, but they had never reached me. I had told her, too, of all that made my happiness; I wrote her about the sweet girl I had seen on shipboard, and how I met her afterward, and what a happy time we passed down in Devon. I even told her of the strange dream I had, in which Isabel seemed to be in England, and to turn away from me sadly because I called " Carry."

I also told her of all I saw in that great world of Paris, writing as I would write to a sister; and I told her, too, of the sweet Roman girl, Enrica, — of her brown hair, and of her rich eyes, and of her pretty Carnival dresses. And when I missed letter after letter, I told her that she must still write her letters, or some little journal, and read it to me when I came back. I thought how pleasant it would be to sit under the trees by her father's house, and listen to her tender voice going through that record of her thoughts and fears. Alas, how our hopes betray us!

It began almost like a diary about the time that her father fell sick. "It is," said she to Lilly, when she gave it to her, "what I would have said to Cousin Paul, if he had been here."

It begins: ". . . I have come back now to father's house; I could not leave him alone, for they told me he was sick. I found him not well; he was very glad to see me, and kissed me so tenderly that I am sure, Cousin Paul, you would not have said. as you used to say, that he was a cold man! I sometimes read to him sitting in the deep library-window, (you remember it,) where we used to nestle out of his sight at dusk. He cannot read any more.

"I would give anything to see the little Carry you speak of; but do you know you did not describe her to me at all; will you not tell me if she has dark hair, or light; or if her eyes are blue, or dark like mine? Is she good; did she not make ugly speeches, or grow peevish, in those long days upon the ocean? How I would have liked to have been with you on those clear starlit nights, looking off upon the water! But then I think that you would not have wished me there, and that you did not once think of me even. This makes me sad; yet I know not why it should, for I always liked you best when you were happy; and I am sure you must have been happy then. You say you shall never see her after you have left the ship: you must not think so, Cousin Paul; if she is so beautiful and fond as you tell me, your own heart will lead you in her way some time again; I feel almost sure of it.

...... "Father is getting more and more feeble, and wandering in his mind; this is very dreadful; he calls me sometimes by my mother's name; and when I say, 'It is Isabel,' he says, 'What Isabel?' and treats me as if I was a stranger. The physician shakes his head when I ask him of father. Oh, Paul! if he should die, what could I do? I should die too; I know I should. Who would there be to care for me? Lilly is married, and Ben is far off, and you, Paul, whom I love better than either, are a long way from me. But God 's good, and he will spare my father.

...... "So you have seen again your little Carry I told you it would be so. You tell me how accidental it was. Ah, Paul, Paul, you rogue! honest as you are, I half doubt you there. I like your description of her too, — dark eyes like mine you say, 'almost as pretty.' Well, Paul, I will forgive you that; it is only a white lie. You know they must be a great deal prettier than mine, or you would never have stayed a whole fortnight in an old farmer's house far down in Devon! I wish I could see her; I wish she was here with you now, for it is midsummer, and the trees and flowers were never prettier But I am all alone; father is too ill to go out at all. I fear now very much that he will never go out again. Lilly was here yesterday, but he did not know her. She read me your last letter; it was not so long as mine. You are very, very good to me, Paul.

...... "For a long time I have written nothing; my father has been very ill, and the old housekeeper has been sick too, and father would have no one but me near him. He cannot live long. I feel sadly, miserably; you will not know me when you come home; your pretty Bella,' as you used to call me, will have lost all her beauty. But perhaps you will not care for that, for you tell me you have found one prettier than ever. I do not know, Cousin Paul, but it is because I am so sad and selfish, — for sorrow is selfish, — but I do not like your raptures about the Roman girl. Be careful, Paul I know your heart; it is quick and sensitive; and I dare say she is pretty, and has beautiful eyes; for they tell me all the Italian girls have soft eyes.

"But Italy is far away, Paul; I can never see Enrica: she will never come here. No, no; remember Devon; I feel as if Carry was a sister now; I cannot feel so of the Roman girl; I do not want to feel so. You will say this is harsh; and I am afraid you will not like me so well for it, but I cannot help saying it. I love you too well, Cousin Paul, not to say it.

. . . . . . "It is all over! Indeed, Paul, I am very desolate! 'The golden bowl is broken;' my poor father has gone to his last home. I was expecting it; but how can we expect that fearful comer — Death? He had been for a long time so feeble that he could scarce speak at all; he sat for hours in his chair, looking upon the fire, or looking out at the window. He would hardly notice me when I came to change his pillows, or to smooth them for his head. But before he died he knew me as well as ever. 'Isabel,' he said, 'you have been a good daughter; God will reward you!' and he kissed me so tenderly, and looked after me so anxiously, with such intelligence in his look, that I thought perhaps he would revive again. In the evening he asked me for one of his books that he loved very much. 'Father,' said I, 'you cannot read; it is almost dark.'

"'Oh, yes,' said he; 'Isabel, I can read now. And I brought it; he kept my hand a long while, then he opened the book; it was a book about death.

"I brought a candle, for I knew he could not read without.

"'Isabel, dear,' said he, 'put the candle a little nearer.' But it was close beside him even then.

"'A little nearer, Isabel,' repeated he, and his voice was very faint, and he grasped my hand hard.

—"'Nearer, Isabel!—nearer!'

"There was no need to do it, for my poor father was dead! Oh! Paul, Paul! pity me. I do not know but I am crazed. It does not seem the same world it was. And the house and the trees! oh, they are very dismal!

"I wish you would come home, Cousin Paul; life would not be so very, very blank as it is now. Lilly is kind; I thank her from my heart. But it is not *her* father who is dead!

. . . . . . "I am calmer now; I am staying with Lilly. The world seems smaller than it did; but heaven seems a great deal larger; there is a place for us all there, Paul, if we only seek it. They tell me you are coming home: I am glad. You will not like, perhaps, to come away from that pretty Enrica you speak of; but do so, Paul. It seems to me that I see clearer than I did, and I talk bolder. The girlish Isabel you will not find, for I am much older, and my air is more grave; and this suffering has made me feeble, very feeble.

...... "It is not easy for me to write; but I must tell you that I have just found out who your Carry is. Years ago, when you were away from home, I was at school with her. We were always together. I wonder I could not have found her out from your description; but I did not even suspect it. She is a dear girl, and is worthy of all your love. I have seen her once since you have met her; we talked of you. She spoke kindly, very kindly; more than this I cannot tell you, for I do not know more. Ah, Paul, may you be happy: I feel as if I had but a little while to live.

...... "It is even so, my dear Cousin Paul: I shall write but little more; my hand trembles now. But I am ready. It is a glorious world beyond this; I know it is! And there we shall meet. I did hope to see you once again, and to hear your voice speaking to me as you used to speak. But I shall not. Life is too frail with me. I seem to live wholly now in the world where I am going; *there* is my mother, and my father, and my little brother; we shall meet, I know we shall meet!

.   . . . . . "The last, Paul. Never again in this world! I am happy, very happy. You will come to me. I can write no more. May good angels guard you, and bring you to heaven!"

—— Shall I go on?

But the toils of life are upon me. Private griefs do not break the force and the weight of the great Present. A life — at best the half of it — is before me. It is to be wrought out with nerve and work. And, blessed be God! there are gleams of sunlight upon it. That sweet Carry — doubly dear to me now that she is joined with my sorrow for the lost Isabel — shall be sought for!

And with her sweet image floating before me, the NOON wanes, and the shadows of EVENING lengthen upon the land.

III.

Evening.

THE Future is a great land: how the lights and the shadows throng over it — bright and dark, slow and swift!

Pride and Ambition build up great castles on its plains, — great monuments on the mountains that reach heavenward, and dip their tops in the blue of Eternity! Then comes an earthquake — the earthquake of disappointment, of distrust, or of inaction — and lays them low. Gaping desolation widens its breaches everywhere; the eye is full of them, and can see nothing beside. By-and-by the sun peeps forth — as now from behind yonder cloud — and reanimates the soul.

Fame beckons, sitting high in the heavens; and joy lends a halo to the vision. A thousand resolves stir your heart; your hand is hot and feverish for action; your brain works madly, and you snatch here, and you snatch there, in the convulsive throes of your delirium Perhaps you see some earnest, careful plodder, once far behind you, now toiling slowly but surely over the plain of life, until he seems near to grasping those brilliant phantoms which dance along the horizon of the future and the sight stirs your soul to frenzy, and you bound on after him with the madness of a fever in your veins. But it was by no such action that the fortunate toiler has won his progress. His hand is steady; his brain is cool; his eye is fixed and sure.

The Future is a great land; a man cannot go round it in a day; he cannot measure it with a bound; he cannot bind its harvests into a single sheaf. It is wider than the vision, and has no end.

Yet always, day by day, hour by hour, second by second, the hard Present is elbowing us off into that great land of the Future. Our souls indeed wander to it as to a home-land; they run beyond time and space, beyond planets and suns, beyond far-off suns and comets, until, like blind flies, they are lost in the blaze of immensity, and can only grope their way back to our earth and our time by the cunning of instinct.

Cut out the Future, even that little Future which is the Evening of our life, and what a fall into vacuity! Forbid those earnest forays over the borders of Now, and on what spoils would the soul live?

For myself, I delight to wander there, and to weave every day the passing life into the coming life — so closely that I may be unconscious of the joining. And if so be that I am able, I would make the whole piece bear fair proportions and just figures, like those taper tries on which nuns work by inches, and finish with their lives; or like those grand frescos which poet-artists have wrought on the vaults of old cathedrals, gaunt and colossal, — appearing mere daubs of carmine and azure, as they lay upon their backs, working out a hand's-breadth at a time, — but when complete, showing — symmetrical and glorious!

But not alone does the soul wander to those glittering heights where Fame sits, with plumes waving in zephyrs of applause; there belong to it other appetites, which range wide and constantly over the broad Future-land. We are not merely working, intellectual machines, but social puzzles, whose solution is the work of a life. Much as hope may lean toward the intoxicating joy of distinction, there is another leaning in the soul, deeper and stronger, toward those pleasures which the heart pants for, and in whose atmosphere the affections bloom and ripen.

The first may indeed be uppermost; it may be noisiest; it may drown with the clamor of mid-day the nicer sympathies. But all our day is not mid-day; and all our life is not noise. Silence is as strong as the soul, and there is no tempest so wild with blasts but has a wilder lull. There lies in the depth of every man's soul a mine of affection, which from time to time will burn with the seething heat of a volcano, and heave up lava-like monuments through all the cold strata of his commoner nature.

One may hide his warmer feelings; he may paint them dimly; he may crowd them out of his sailing-chart, where he only sets down the harbors for traffic; yet in his secret heart he will map out upon the great country of the Future fairy islands of love and of joy. There he will be sure to wander, when his soul is lost in those quiet and hallowed hopes which take hold on heaven.

Love only unlocks the door upon that Futurity where the isles of the blessed lie like stars. Affection is the stepping-stone to God. The heart is our only measure of infinitude. The mind tires with greatness; the heart — never. Thought is worried and weakened in its flight through the immensity of space, but Love soars around the throne of the Highest with added blessing and strength.

I know not how it may be with others, but with me the heart is a readier and quicker builder of those fabrics which strew the great country of the Future than the mind. They may not, indeed, rise so high as the dizzy pinnacles that ambition loves to rear; but they lie like fragrant islands in a sea whose ripple is a continuous melody.

And as I muse now, looking toward the Evening, which is already begun, — tossed as I am with the toils of the Past, and bewildered with the vexations of the Present, — my affections are the architect that build up the future refuge. And in fancy at least I will build it boldly, saddened it may be by the chance shadows of evening; but through all I will hope for a sunset, when the day ends, glorious with crimson and gold.

Carry.

I SAID that, harsh and hot as was the Present, there were joyous gleams of light playing over the Future. How else could it be when that fair being whom I met first upon the wastes of ocean, and whose name even is hallowed by the dying words of Isabel, is living in the same world with me? Amid all the perplexities that haunt me as I wander from the present to the future, the thought of her image, of her smile, of her last kind adieu, throws a dash of sunlight upon my path.

And yet why? Is it not very idle? Years have passed since I have seen her; I do not even know where she may be. What is she to me?

My heart whispers, "Very much!"—but I do not listen to that in my prouder moods. She is a woman, a beautiful woman indeed, whom I have known once—pleasantly known; she is living, but she will die, or she will marry: I shall hear of it by-and-by, and sigh perhaps,—nothing more. Life is earnest around me there is no time to delve in the past, for bright things to shed radiance on the future.

I will forget the sweet girl who was with me upon the ocean, and think she is dead. This manly soul is strong, if we would but think so; it can make a puppet of griefs, and take down and set up at will the symbols of its hope.

—— But no, I cannot; the more I think thus, the less I really think thus. A single smile of that frail girl — when I recall it — mocks all my proud purposes, as if without her my purposes were nothing.

———— Pshaw! I say, it is idle; and I bury my thought in books, and in long hours of toil; but, as the hours lengthen, and my head sinks with fatigue, and the shadows of evening play around me, there comes again that sweet vision, saying with tender mockery, "Is it idle?" And I am helpless, and am led away hopefully and joyfully toward the golden gates which open on the Future.

But this is only in those silent hours when the man is alone and away from his working thoughts. At midday, or in the rush of the world, he puts hard armor on, that reflects all the light of such joyous fancies. He is cold and careless, and ready for suffering and for fight.

One day I am travelling. I am absorbed in some present cares, thinking out some plan which is to make easier or more successful the voyage of life. I glance upon the passing scenery, and upon new faces, with that careless indifference which grows upon a man with years, and above all with travel. There is no wife to enlist your sympathies, no children to sport with; my friends are few and scattered, and are working out fairly what is before them to do. Lilly is living here, and Ben is living there; their letters are cheerful, contented letters, and they wish me well. Griefs even have grown light with wearing; and I am just in that careless humor as if I said, Jog on, old world,—jog on! And the end will come along soon, and we shall get — poor devils that we are — just what we deserve.

But on a sudden my eyes rest on a figure that I think I know. Now the indifference flies like mist; and my heart throbs, and the old visions come up. I watch her, as if there were nothing else to be seen. The form is hers; the grace is hers; the simple dress,— so neat, so tasteful!—that is hers too. She half turns her head: it is the face that I saw under the velvet cap in the Park of Devon!

I do not rush forward; I sit as if I were in a trance I watch her every action,— the kind attentions to her mother, who sits beside her,— her naive exclamations as we pass some point of surpassing beauty. It seems as if a new world were opening to me; yet I cannot tell why. I keep my place, and think, and gaze. I tear the paper I hold in my hand into shreds. I play with my watch-chain, and twist the seal until it is near breaking.

I take out my watch, look at it, and put it back; yet I cannot tell the hour.

—— It is she, I murmur; I know it is Carry!

But when they rise to leave, my lethargy is broken; yet it is with a trembling hesitation — a faltering as it were between the present life and the future — that I approach. She knows me on the instant, and greets me kindly; as Bella wrote — very kindly. Yet she shows a slight embarrassment, a sweet embarrassment, that I treasure in my heart more closely even than the greeting. I change my course, and travel with them; now we talk of the old scenes, and two hours seem to have made with me the difference of half a lifetime.

It is five years since I parted with her, never hoping to meet again. She was then a frail girl; she is now just rounding into womanhood. Her eyes are as dark and deep as ever; the lashes that fringe them seem to me even longer than they were. Her color is as rich, her forehead as fair, her smile as sweet, as they were before; only a little tinge of sadness floats upon her eye, like the haze upon a summer landscape. I grow bold to look upon her, and timid with looking. We talk of Bella: she speaks in a soft, low voice, and the shade of sadness on her face gathers, as when a summer mist obscures the sun. I talk in monosyllables; I can command no other. And there is a look of sympathy in her eye, when I speak thus, that binds my soul to her as no smiles could do. What can draw the heart into the fulness of love so quick as sympathy?

But this passes; we must part: she for her home, and I for that broad home that has been mine so long — the world. It seems broader to me than ever, and colder than ever, and less to be wished for than ever. A new book of hope is sprung wide open in my life: a hope of home!

We are to meet at some time, not far off, in the city where I am living. I look forward to that time as at school I used to look for vacation; it is a *point d'appui* for hope, for thought, and for countless journeyings into the opening future. Never did I keep the dates better, never count the days more carefully, whether for bonds to be paid, or for dividends to fall due.

I welcome the time, and it passes like a dream. I am near her, often as I dare; the hours are very short with her, and very long away. She receives me kindly — always very kindly; she could not be otherwise than kind. But is it anything more? This is a greedy nature of ours; and when sweet kindness flows upon us, we want more. I know she is kind; and yet in place of being grateful, I am only covetous of an excess of kindness.

She does not mistake my feelings, surely, — ah, no, — trust a woman for that! But what have I, or what am I, to ask a return? She is pure and gentle as an angel;

and I, alas, only a poor soldier in our world-fight against the Devil! Sometimes, in moods of vanity, I call up what I fondly reckon my excellencies or deserts,— a sorry, pitiful array, that makes me shamefaced when I meet her. And in an instant I banish them all. And I think, that, if I were called upon in some high court of justice to say why I should claim her indulgence, or her love, I would say nothing of my sturdy effort to beat down the roughnesses of toil, — nothing of such manliness as wears a calm front amid the frowns of the world, — nothing of little triumphs in the every-day fight of life; but only, I would enter the simple plea — this heart is hers!

She leaves; and I have said nothing of what was seething within me: how I curse my folly! She is gone, and never perhaps will return. I recall in despair her last kind glance. The world seems blank to me. She does not know, perhaps she does not care, if I love her. Well, I will bear it, I say. But I cannot bear it. Business is broken; books are blurred; something remains undone that fate declares must be done. Not a place can I find, but her sweet smile gives to it either a tinge of gladness, or a black shade of desolation.

I sit down at my table with pleasant books; the fire is burning cheerfully; my dog looks up earnestly when I speak to him; but it will never do! Her image sweeps away all these comforts in a flood. I fling down my book; I turn my back upon my dog; the fire hisses and sparkles in mockery of me.

Suddenly a thought flashes on my brain: I will write to her, I say. And a smile floats over my face, — a smile of hope, ending in doubt. I catch up my pen — my trusty pen; and the clean sheet lies before me. The paper could not be better, nor the pen. I have written hundreds of letters; it is easy to write letters; but now it is not easy.

I begin, and cross it out. I begin again, and get on a little farther; then cross it out. I try again, but can write nothing. I fling down my pen in despair, and burn the sheet, and go to my library for some old sour treatise of Shaftesbury or Lyttleton; and say, — talking to myself all the while, — let her go! She is beautiful, but I am strong; the world is short; we — I and my dog, and my books, and my pen — will battle it through bravely, and leave enough for a tombstone.

But even as I say it, the tears start; it is all false saying! And I throw Shaftesbury across the room, and take up my pen again. It glides on and on, as my hope glows, and I tell her of our first meeting, and of our hours in the ocean twilight, and of our unsteady stepping on the heaving deck, and of that parting in the noise of London, and of my joy at seeing her in the pleasant country, and of my grief afterward. And then

I mention Bella,— her friend and mine,— and the tears flow; and then I speak of our last meeting, and of my doubts; and of this very evening; and how I could not write, and abandoned it; and then felt something within me that made me write and tell her — all! — "That my heart was not my own, but was wholly hers; and that if she would be mine — I would cherish her and love her always!"

Then I feel a kind of happiness — a strange, tumultuous happiness, into which doubt is creeping from time to time, bringing with it a cold shudder. I seal the letter, and carry it — a great weight — for the mail It seems as if there could be no other letter that day, and as if all the coaches and horses, and cars, and boats were specially detailed to bear that single sheet. It is a great letter for me; my destiny lies in it.

I do not sleep well that night; it is a tossing sleep One time, joy, sweet and holy joy, comes to my dreams, and an angel is by me; another time, the angel fades, the brightness fades, and I wake struggling with fear. For many nights it is so, until the day comes on which I am looking for a reply.

The postman has little suspicion that the letter which he gives me — although it contains no promissory notes, nor moneys, nor deeds, nor articles of trade — is yet to have a greater influence upon my life and upon my future, than all the letters he has ever brought to me before. But I do not show him this; nor do I let him see the clutch with which I grasp it. I bear it, as if it were a great and fearful burden, to my room. I lock the door, and having broken the seal with a quivering hand, read: —

The Letter.

"PAUL, — for I think I may call you so now, — I know not how to answer you. Your letter gave me great joy; but it gave me pain too. I cannot — will not doubt what you say: I believe that you love me better than I deserve to be loved; and I know that I am not worthy of all your kind praises. But it is not this that pains me; for I know that you have a generous heart, and would forgive, as you always have forgiven, any weakness of mine. I am proud too, very proud, to have won your love; but it pains me — more perhaps than you will believe — to think that I cannot write back to you as I would wish to write; alas, never!"

Here I dash the letter upon the floor, and, with my hand upon my forehead, sit gazing upon the glowing coals, and breathing quick and loud. The dream then is broken!

Presently I read again: —

—— " You know that my father died before we had ever met. He had an old friend who had come from England, and who in early life had done him some great service, which made him seem like a brother. This old gentleman was my godfather, and called me daughter. When my father died, he drew me to his side and said, ' Carry, I shall leave you, but my old friend will be your father ; ' and he put my hand in his and said, ' I give you my daughter.'

" This old gentleman had a son, older than myself; but we were much together, and grew up as brother and sister. I was proud of him, for he was tall and strong, and every one called him handsome. He was as kind, too, as a brother could be ; and his father was like my own father. Every one said and believed that we would one day be married ; and my mother and my new father spoke of it openly. So did Laurence, for that is my friend's name.

" I do not need to tell you any more, Paul ; for when I was still a girl, we had promised that we would one day be man and wife. Laurence has been much in England ; and I believe he is there now. The old gentleman treats me still as a daughter, and talks of the time when I shall come and live with him. The letters of Laurence are very kind ; and though he does not talk so much of our marriage as he did, it is only, I think, because he regards it as so certain.

I have wished to tell you all this before, but I have feared to tell you; I am afraid I have been too selfish to tell you. And now what can I say? Laurence seems most to me like a brother; and you, Paul — but I must not go on. For if I marry Laurence, as fate seems to have decided, I will try and love him better than all the world.

"But will you not be a brother, and love me as you once loved Bella? You say my eyes are like hers, and that my forehead is like hers: will you not believe that my heart is like hers too?

"Paul, if you shed tears over this letter, I have shed them as well as you. I can write no more now.
"Adieu."

I sit long, looking upon the blaze; and when I rouse myself it is to say wicked things against destiny. Again all the future seems very blank. I cannot love Carry as I loved Bella; she cannot be a sister to me; she must be more, or nothing! Again, I seem to float singly on the tide of life, and see all around me in cheerful groups. Everywhere the sun shines, except upon my own cold forehead. There seems no mercy in heaven, and no goodness for me upon earth.

I write, after some days, an answer to the letter. But it is a bitter answer, in which I forget myself — in the whirl of my misfortunes — to the utterance of reproaches.

Her reply, which comes speedily, is sweet and gentle She is hurt by my reproaches, deeply hurt. But with a touching kindness, of which I am not worthy, she credits all my petulance to my wounded feeling; she soothes me, but in soothing only wounds the more. I try to believe her when she speaks of her unworthiness, but I cannot.

Business, and the pursuits of ambition or of interest, pass on like dull, grating machinery. Tasks are met and performed, with strength indeed, but with no cheer. Courage is high, as I meet the shocks and trials of the world; but it is a brute, careless courage, that glories in opposition. I laugh at any dangers, or any insidious pitfalls; what are they to me? What do I possess which it will be hard to lose? My dog keeps by me; my toils are present; my food is ready; my limbs are strong: — what need for more?

The months slip by; and the cloud that floated over my evening sun passes.

Laurence, wandering abroad and writing to Caroline as to a sister, writes more than his father could have wished. He has met new faces, very sweet faces, and one which shows through the ink of his later letters very gorgeously. The old gentleman does not like to lose thus his little Carry, and he writes back rebuke. But Laurence, with the letters of Caroline before him for data, throws himself upon his sister's kindness and charity. It astonishes not a little the old gentleman to find his daughter pleading in such strange way for the son. "And what will you do then, my Carry?" the old man says.

—— "Wear weeds, if you wish, sir; and love you and Laurence more than ever!"

And he takes her to his bosom, and says, "Carry Carry, you are too good for that wild fellow, Laurence!"

Now the letters are different! Now they are full of hope, dawning all over the future sky. Business, and care, and toil glide as if a spirit animated them all; it is no longer cold machine-work, but intelligent and hopeful activity. The sky hangs upon you lovingly, and the birds make music that startles you with its fineness. Men wear cheerful faces; the storms have a kind pity gleaming through all their wrath.

The days approach when you can call her yours. For she has said it, and her mother has said it; and the kind old gentleman, who says he will still be her father, has said it too; and they have all welcomed you — won by her story — with a cordiality that has made your cup full to running over. Only one thought comes up to obscure your joy: Is it real? or, if real, are you worthy to enjoy? Will you cherish and love always, as you have promised, that angel who accepts your word, and rests her happiness on your faith? Are there not harsh qualities in your nature which you fear may sometime make her regret that she gave herself to your love and charity? And those friends who watch over her as the apple of their eye, can you always meet their tenderness and approval for your guardianship of their treasure? Is it not a treasure that makes you fearful as well as joyful?

But you forget this in her smile; her kindness, her goodness, her modesty will not let you remember it. She *forbids* such thoughts; and you yield such obedience as you never yielded even to the commands of a mother. And if your business and your labor slip by partially neglected, what matters it? What is interest, or what is reputation, compared with that fulness of your heart which is now ripe with joy?

The day for your marriage comes, and you live as if you were in a dream. You think well and hope well for all the world. A flood of charity seems to radiate from all around you. And as you sit beside her in the twilight, on the evening before the day when you will call her yours, and talk of the coming hopes, and of the soft shadows of the past; and whisper of Bella's love, and of that sweet sister's death; and of Laurence, a new brother, coming home joyful with his bride; and lay your cheek to hers,—life seems as if it were all day and as if there could be no night!

The marriage passes, and she is yours,— yours for ever.

New Travel.

AGAIN I am upon the sea, but not alone. She, whom I first met upon the wastes of ocean, is there beside me. Again I steady her tottering step upon the deck; once it was a drifting, careless pleasure; now the pleasure is holy.

Once the fear I felt — as the storms gathered, and night came, and the ship tossed madly, and great waves gathering swift and high came down like slipping mountains, and spent their force upon the quivering vessel — was a selfish fear. But it is so no longer. Indeed I hardly know fear; for how can the tempests harm *her?* Is she not too good to suffer any of the wrath of heaven?

And in nights of calm — holy nights — we lean over the ship's side, looking down, as once before, into the dark depths, and murmur again snatches of ocean song, and talk of those we love; and we peer among the stars, which seem neighborly, and as if they were the homes of friends. And as the great ocean-swells come rocking under us, and carry us up and down along the valleys and the hills of water, they seem like deep pulsations of the great heart of nature, heaving us forward onward the goal of life, and to the gates of heaven!

We watch the ships as they come upon the horizon

and sweep toward us, like false friends, with the sun glittering on their sails; and then shift their course, and bear away — with their bright sails turned to spots of shadow. We watch the long-winged birds skimming the waves hour after hour, like pleasant thoughts; now dashing before our bows, and then sweeping behind, until they are lost in the hollows of the water.

Again life lies open, as it did once before; but the regrets, disappointments, and fruitless resolves do not come to trouble me now. It is the future, which has become as level as the sea; and *she* is beside me, the sharer in that future, to look out with me upon the joyous sparkle of water, and to count with me the dazzling ripples that lie between us and the shore. A thousand pleasant plans come up, and are abandoned, like the waves we leave behind us; a thousand other joyous plans dawn upon our fancy, like the waves that glitter before us. We talk of Laurence and his bride, whom we are to meet; we talk of her mother, who is even now watching the winds that waft her child over the ocean; we talk of the kindly old man, her godfather, who gave her a father's blessing; we talk low, and in the twilight hours, of Isabel — who sleeps.

At length, as the sun goes down upon a fair night over the western waters which we have passed, we see before us the low, blue line of the shores of Cornwall and Devon. In the night, shadowy ships glide past us with gleaming lanterns; and in the morning we see the yellow cliffs of the Isle of Wight, and standing out from the land is the dingy sail of our pilot. London, with its fog, roar, and crowds, has not the same charms that it once had; that roar and crowd is good to make a man forget his griefs, forget himself, and stupefy him with amazement. We are in no need of such forgetfulness.

We roll along the banks of the sylvan river that glides by Hampton Court; and we toil up Richmond Hill, to look together upon that scene of water and meadow, — of leafy copses, and glistening villas, — of brown cottages, and clustered hamlets, — of solitary oaks, and loitering herds, — all spread like a veil of beauty upon the bosom of the Thames. But we cannot linger here, nor even under the glorious old boles of Windsor Forest; but we hurry on to that sweet county of Devon, made green with its white skeins of water.

Again we loiter under the oaks where we have loitered before; and the sleek deer gaze on us with their liquid eyes, as they gazed before. The squirrels sport among the boughs as fearless as ever; and some wandering puss pricks her long ears at our steps, and bounds off along the hedge-rows to her burrow. Again I see Carry in her velvet riding-cap, with the white plume; and I meet her, as I met her before, under the princely trees that skirt the northern avenue. I recall the evening when I sauntered out at the park-gates, and gained a blessing from the porter's wife, and dreamed that strange dream;— now, the dream seems more real than my life. " God bless you!" said the woman again.

—" Aye, old lady, God has blessed me!"—and I fling her a guinea, not as a gift, but as a debt.

The bland farmer lives yet; he scarce knows me, until I tell him of my bout around his oatfield at the tail of his long-stilted plough. I find the old pew in the parish church. Other holly-sprigs are hung now; and I do not doze, for Carry is beside me. The curate drawls the service, but it is pleasant to listen; and I make the responses with an emphasis that tells more, I fear, for my joy than for my religion. The old groom at the mansion in the Park has not forgotten the hard riding of other days, and tells long stories (to which I love to listen) of the old visit of Mistress Carry, when she followed the hounds with the best of the English lasses.

—" Yer honor may well be proud, for not a prettier face, or a kinder heart, has been in Devon since Mistress Carry left us!"

But pleasant as are the old woods, full of memories, and pleasant as are the twilight evenings upon the terrace, we must pass over to the mountains of Switzerland. There we are to meet Laurence.

EVENING. 263

Carry has never seen the magnificence of the Juras; and as we journey over the hills between Dole and the border line, looking upon the rolling heights shrouded with pine-trees, and down thousands of feet, at the very road-side, upon the cottage-roofs, and emerald valleys, where the dun herds are feeding quietly, she is lost in admiration. At length we come to that point above the little town of Gex, from which you see, spread out before you, the meadows that skirt Geneva, the placid surface of Lake Leman, and the rough, shaggy mountains of Savoy; and far behind them, breaking the horizon with snowy cap, and with dark pinnacles, Mont Blanc, and the Needles of Chamouni.

I point out to her in the valley below the little town of Ferney, where stands the deserted *chateau* of Voltaire; and beyond, upon the shores of the lake, the old home of De Staël; and across, with its white walls reflected upon the bosom of the water, the house where Byron wrote the "Prisoner of Chillon." Among the grouping roofs of Geneva we trace the dark cathedral, and the tall hotels shining on the edge of the lake. And I tell of the time when I tramped down through yonder valley, with my future all visionary and broken, and drank the splendor of the scene, only as a quick relief to the monotony of my solitary life.

—— "And now, Carry, with your hand locked in mine, and your heart mine, yonder lake sleeping in the sun, and the snowy mountains with their rosy hue, seem like the smile of Nature, bidding us be glad!"

Laurence is at Geneva: he welcomes Carry as he would welcome a sister. He is a noble fellow, and tells me much of his sweet Italian wife; and presents me to the smiling, blushing — Enrica! She has learned English now; she has found, she says, a better teacher than ever I was. Yet she welcomes me warmly, as a sister might; and we talk of those old evenings by the blazing fire, and of the one-eyed *Maestro*, as children, long separated, might talk of their school-tasks and of their teachers. She cannot tell me enough of her praises of Laurence, and of his noble heart. "You were good," she says, "but Laurence is better."

Carry admires her soft brown hair, and her deep liquid eye, and wonders how I could ever have left Rome?

——— Do you indeed wonder, Carry?

And together we go down into Savoy, to that marvellous valley which lies under the shoulder of Mont Blanc; and we wander over the *Mer de Glace*, and pick Alpine roses from the edge of the frowning glacier. We toil at nightfall up to the monastery of the Great St. Bernard, where the new-forming ice crackles in the narrow footway, and the cold moon glistens over wastes of snow, and upon the windows of the dark Hospice. Again, we are among the granite heights, whose ledges are filled with ice, upon the Grimsel. The pond is dark and cold; the paths are slippery; the great glacier of Aar sends down icy breezes, and the echoes ring from rock to rock, as if the ice-god answered. And yet we neither suffer nor fear. .

In the sweet valley of Meyringen we part from Laurence: he goes northward, by Grindenwald and Thun, thence to journey westward, and to make for the Roman girl a home beyond the ocean. Enrica bids me go on to Rome: she knows that Carry will love its soft, warm air, its ruins, its pictures and temples, better than these cold valleys of Switzerland. And she gives me kind messages for her mother, and for Cesare; and should we be in Rome at the Easter season, she bids us remember her, when we listen to the *Miserere*, and when we see the great *Chiesa* on fire, and when we saunter upon the Pincian Hill, — and remember that it is her home.

We follow them with our eyes as they go up the steep height over which falls the white foam of the clattering Reichenbach; and they wave their hands toward us, and disappear upon the little plateau which stretches toward the crystal Rosenlaui, and the tall, still Engel-Hörner.

May the mountain angels guard them!

As we journey on toward that wonderful pass of Splügen, I recall by the way, upon the heights and in the valleys, the spots where I lingered years before Here, I plucked a flower; there, I drank from that cold, yellow glacier water; and here, upon some rock overlooking a stretch of broken mountains, hoary with their eternal frosts, I sat musing upon that very Future which is with me now. But never, even when the ice genii were most prodigal of their fancies to the wanderer, did I look for more joy, or a better angel.

Afterward, when all our trembling upon the Alpine paths has gone by, we are rolling along under the chestnuts and lindens that skirt the banks of Como. We recall that sweet story of Manzoni, and I point out, as well as I may, the loitering place of the *bravi*, and the track of poor Don Abbondio. We follow in the path of the discomfited Renzi, to where the dainty spire and pinnacles of the Duomo of Milan glisten against the violet sky.

Carry longs to see Venice; its water-streets and palaces have long floated in her visions. In the bustling activity of our own country, and in the quiet fields of England, that strange, half-deserted capital, lying in the Adriatic, has taken the strongest hold upon her fancy.

So we leave Padua and Verona behind us, and find ourselves upon a soft spring noon upon the end of the iron road which stretches across the lagoon toward Venice. With the hissing of steam in the ear, it is hard to think of the wonderful city we are approaching. But as we escape from the carriage, and set our feet down into one of those strange, hearse-like, ancient boats, with its sharp iron prow, and listen to the melodious, rolling tongue of the Venetian gondolier; — as we see rising over the watery plain before us — all glittering in the sun — tall, square towers with pyramidal tops, and clustered domes, and minarets, and sparkling roofs lifting from marble walls, — all so like the old paintings; — and as we glide nearer and nearer to the floating wonder under the silent working oar of our now silent gondolier; — as we ride up swiftly under the deep, broad shadows of palaces, and see plainly the play of the sea-water in the crevices of the masonry, and turn into narrow rivers shaded darkly by overhanging walls, hearing no sound but of voices, or the swaying of the water against the houses, — we feel the presence of the place. And the mystic fingers of the Past, grappling our spirits, lead them away, willing and rejoicing captives, through the long vista of the ages that are gone.

Carry is in a trance, — rapt by the witchery of the scene into dream. This is her Venice; nor have all the visions, that played upon her fancy, been equal to the enchanting presence of this hour of approach.

Afterward it becomes a living thing, stealing upon the affections and upon the imagination by a thousand coy advances. We wander, under the warm Italian sunlight to the steps from which rolled the white head of poor Marino Faliero. The gentle Carry can now thrust her ungloved hand into the terrible Lion's mouth. We enter the *salon* of the fearful Ten, and peep through the half-opened door into the cabinet of the more fearful Three. We go through the deep dungeons of Carmagnola and of Carrara; and we instruct the willing gondolier to push his dark boat under the Bridge of Sighs; and, with Rogers's poem in our hand, glide up to the prison-door, and read of

> " that fearful closet at the foot
> Lurking for prey, which, when a victim came,
> Grew less and less, contracting to a span
> An iron door, urged onward by a screw,
> Forcing out life!"

I sail, listening to nothing but the dip of the gondolier's oar, or to *her* gentle words, fast under the palace-door which closed that fearful morning on the guilt and shame of Bianca Capello. Or, with souls lit up by the scene into a buoyancy that can scarce distinguish between what is real and what is merely written, we chase the anxious step of the forsaken Corinna; or seek among the veteran palaces the casement of the old Brabantio, — the chamber of Desdemona, — the house of Jessica; and trace among the strange Jew money-changers, who yet haunt the Rialto, the likeness of the bearded Shylock. We wander into stately churches.

brushing over grass or tell-tale flowers that grow in the court, and find them damp and cheerless; the incense rises murkily, and rests in a thick cloud over the altars, and over the paintings; the music, if so be that the organ-notes are swelling under the roof, is mournfully plaintive.

Of an afternoon we sail over to the Lido, to gladden our eyes with a sight of land and green things, and we pass none upon the way save silent oarsmen, with barges piled high with the produce of their gardens, pushing their way down toward the floating city. And upon the narrow island we find Jewish graves, half covered by drifted sand; and from among them watch the sunset glimmering over a desolate level of water. As we glide back, lights lift over the Lagoon, and double along the Guideca and the Grand Canal. The little neighbor isles will have their company of lights dancing in the water; and from among them will rise up against the mellow evening sky of Italy, gaunt, unlighted houses.

After the nightfall, which brings no harmful dew with it, I stroll, with her hand within my arm, — as once upon the sea, and in the English Park, and in the homeland, — over that great square which lies before the palace of St. Mark's. The white moon is riding in the middle heaven like a globe of silver; the gondoliers stride over the echoing stones; and their long, black shadows, stretching over the pavement, or shaking upon the moving water, seem like great funereal plumes waving over the bier of Venice.

Carrying thence whole treasures of thought and fancy to feed upon in the after-years, we wander to Rome.

I find the old one-eyed *maestro*, and am met with cordial welcome by the mother of the pretty Enrica. The Count has gone to the Marches of Ancona. Lame Pietro still shuffles around the boards at the Lepré, and the flower-sellers at the corner bind me a more brilliant bouquet than ever for a new beauty at Rome. As we ramble under the broken arches of the great aqueduct stretching toward Frascati, I tell Carry the story of my trip in the Apennines, and we search for the pretty Carlotta. But she is married, they tell us, to a Neapolitan guardsman. In the spring twilight we wander upon those heights which lie between Frascati and Albano, and, looking westward, see that glorious view of the Campagna which can never be forgotten. But beyond the Campagna, and beyond the huge hulk of St. Peter's, heaving into the sky from the middle waste, we see — or fancy we see — a glimpse of the sea which stretches out and on to the land we love better than Rome. And in fancy we build up that home which shall belong to us on the return, — a home that has slumbered long in the future, and which, now that the future has come, lies fairly before me.

Home.

YEARS seem to have passed. They have mellowed life into ripeness. The start, and change, and hot ambition of youth seem to have gone by. A calm and joyful quietude has succeeded. That future, which still lies before me, seems like a roseate twilight sinking into a peaceful and silent night.

My home is a cottage near that where Isabel once lived. The same valley is around me; the same brook rustles and loiters under the gnarled roots of the overhanging trees. The cottage is no mock cottage, but a substantial, wide-spreading cottage, with clustering gables and ample shade, — such a cottage as they build upon the slopes of Devon. Vines clamber over it, and the stones show mossy through the interlacing climbers. There are low porches with cosy arm-chairs, and generous oriels fragrant with mignonette and the blue blossoming violets.

The chimney-stacks rise high, and show clear against the heavy pine-trees that ward off the blasts of winter. The dove-cote is a habited dove-cote, and the purple-necked pigeons swoop around the roofs in great companies. The hawthorn is budding into its June fragrance along all the lines of fence, and the paths are trim and clean. The shrubs — our neglected azalias and rhododendrons chiefest among them — stand in picturesque groups upon the close-shaven lawn.

The gateway in the thicket below is between two mossy old posts of stone; and there is a tall hemlock, flanked by a sturdy pine, for sentinel. Within the cottage the library is wainscoted with native oak; and my trusty gun hangs upon a branching pair of antlers. M rod and nets are disposed above the generous book shelves; and a stout eagle, once a tenant of the native woods, sits perched over the central alcove. An old-fashioned mantel is above the brown stone jambs of the country fireplace, and along it are distributed records of travel, — little bronze temples from Rome, the *pietro duro* of Florence, the porcelain busts of Dresden, the rich iron of Berlin, and a cup fashioned from a stag's horn, from the Black Forest by the Rhine.

Massive chairs stand here and there in tempting attitude; strewed over an oaken table in the middle are the uncut papers and volumes of the day; and upon a lion's skin stretched before the hearth is lying another Tray.

But this is not all. There are children in the cottage. There is Jamie; — we think him handsome, for he has the dark hair of his mother, and the same black eye with its long, heavy fringe. There is Carry — little Carry I must call her now, — with a face full of glee, and rosy with health. Then there is a little rogue some two years old, whom we call Paul, — a very bad boy, as we tell him.

The mother is as beautiful as ever, and far more dear to me; for gratitude has been adding, year by year, to love. There have been times when a harsh word of mine, uttered in the fatigues of business, has touched her; and I have seen that soft eye fill with tears; and I have upbraided myself for causing her one pang. But such things she does not remember, — or remembers only to cover with her gentle forgiveness.

Laurence and Enrica are living near us. And the old gentleman, who was Carry's godfather, sits with me on sunny days upon the porch, and takes little Paul upon his knee, and wonders if two such daughters as Enrica and Carry are to be found in the world. At twilight we ride over to see Laurence: Jamie mounts with the coachman; little Carry puts on her wide-rimmed Leghorn for the evening visit; and the old gentleman's plea for Paul cannot be denied. The mother too is with us; and old Tray comes whisking along, now frolicking before the horses' heads, and then bounding off after the flight of some belated bird.

Away from that cottage home I seem away from life. Within it, that broad and shadowy future, which lay before me in boyhood and in youth, is garnered, like a fine mist gathered into drops of crystal.

And when away, those long letters, dating from the

cottage home, are what tie me to life. That cherished wife — far dearer to me now than when she wrote that first letter, which seemed a dark veil between me and the future — writes me now as tenderly as then. She narrates, in her delicate way, all the incidents of the home-life; she tells me of their rides, and of their games, and of the new-planted trees, — of all their sunny days, and of their frolics on the lawn; she tell me how Jamie is studying, and of little Carry's beauty, growing every day, and of roguish Paul — so like his father! And she sends me a kiss from each of them; and bids me such adieu, and such " God's blessing," that it seems as if an angel guarded me.

But this is not all; for Jamie has written a postscript.

—— " Dear Father," he says, " mother wishes me to tell you how I am studying. What would you think, father, to have me talk in French to you, when you come back? I wish you would come back though; the hawthorns are coming out, and the apricot under my window is all full of blossoms. If you should bring me a present, as you almost always do, I would like a fishing-rod.

" Your affectionate son,

" JAMIE."

And little Carry has her fine, rambling characters running into a second postscript.

"Why don't you come, papa; you stay too long. I have ridden the pony twice; once he most threw me off. This is all from   CARRY."

And Paul has taken the pen too, and in his extraordinary effort to make a big P, has made a very big blot. And Jamie writes under it, — "This is Paul's work, Pa; but he says it's a love-blot, only he loves you ten hundred times more."

And after your return, Jamie will insist that you should go with him to the brook, and sit down with him upon a tuft of the brake, to fling off a line into the eddies, though only the nibbling roach are sporting below. You have instructed the workmen to spare the clumps of bank-willows, that the wood-duck may have a covert in winter, and that the Bob-o-Lincolns may have a quiet nesting-place in the spring.

Sometimes your wife — too kind to deny such favor — will stroll with you along the meadow banks, and you pick meadow-daisies in memory of the old time. Little Carry weaves them into rude chaplets, to dress the forehead of Paul; and they dance along the greensward, and switch off the daffodils, and blow away the dande-'ion seeds, to see if their wishes are to come true Jamie holds a buttercup under Carry's chin, to find if she loves gold; and Paul, the rogue, teases them by sticking a thistle into sister's curls.

The pony has hard work to do under Carry's swift riding; but he is fed by her own hand with the cold breakfast-rolls. The nuts are gathered in time, and stored for long winter evenings, when the fire is burning bright and cheerily, — a true, hickory blaze, which sends its waving gleams over eager, smiling faces, and over well-stored book-shelves and portraits of dear lost ones. While from time to time that wife, who is the soul of the scene, will break upon the children's prattle, with the silver melody of her voice, running softly and sweetly through the couplets of Crabbe's stories, or the witchery of the Flodden Tale.

Then the boys will guess conundrums, and play at fox-and-geese; and Tray, cherished in his age, and old Milo, petted in his dotage, lie side by side upon the lion's skin before the blazing hearth. Little Tomtit — the goldfinch — sits sleeping on his perch, or cocks his eye at a sudden crackling of the fire for a familiar squint upon our family group.

But there is no future without its straggling clouds. Even now a shadow is trailing along the landscape.

It is a soft and mild day of summer. The leaves are at their fullest. A southern breeze has been blowing up the valley all the morning, and the light, smoky haze hangs in the distant mountain-gaps like a veil on beauty. Jamie has been busy with his lessons, and afterward playing with Milo upon the lawn. Little Carry has come in from a long ride, — her face blooming, and her eyes all smiles and joy. The mother has busied herself with those flowers she loves so well. Little Paul, they say, has been playing in the meadow, and old Tray has gone with him.

But at dinner-time, Paul does not come back.

"Paul ought not to ramble off so far," I say.

The mother says nothing; but there is a look of anxiety upon her face that disturbs me. Jamie wonders where Paul can be, and he saves for him — whatever he knows Paul will like — a heaping plateful. But the dinner-hour passes, and Paul does not come. Old Tray lies in the sunshine by the porch.

Now the mother is indeed anxious. And I, though I conceal this from her, find my fears strangely active. Something like instinct guides me to the meadow; I wander down the brook-side, calling — Paul! Paul! But there is no answer.

All the afternoon we search, and the neighbors search; but it is a fruitless toil. There is no joy that evening: the meal passes in silence; only little Carry, with tears in her eyes, asks if Paul will soon come back. All the night we search and call: the mother even, braving the night-air, and running here and there, until the morning finds us sad and despairing.

That day — the next — cleared up the mystery; but cleared it up with darkness. Poor little Paul! he has sunk under the murderous eddies of the brook! His boyish prattle, his rosy smiles, his artless talk, are lost to us forever!

I will not tell how, nor when, we found him; nor will tell of our desolate home, and of *her* grief — the first crushing grief of her life.

The cottage is still. The servants glide noiseless, as if they might startle the poor little sleeper. The house seems cold, very cold. Yet it is summer weather; and the south breeze plays softly along the meadow, and softly over the murderous eddies of the brook.

Then comes the hush of burial. The kind mourners are there; — it is easy for them to mourn! The good clergyman prays by the bier: — "O Thou, who didst take upon thyself human woe, and drank deep of every pang in life, let thy Spirit come and heal this grief, and guide toward that Better Land, where justice and love shall reign, and hearts laden with anguish shall rest forevermore!"

Weeks roll on; and a smile of resignation lights up the saddened features of the mother. Those dark mourning-robes speak to the heart deeper and more tenderly than even the bridal costume. She lightens the weight of your grief by her sweet words of resignation. "Paul," she says, "God has taken our boy!"

Other weeks roll on. Joys are still left — great and ripe joys. The cottage smiling in the autumn sunshine is there; the birds are in the forest boughs; Jamie and little Carry are there; and she, who is more than them all, is cheerful and content. Heaven has taught us that the brightest future has its clouds, that this life is a motley of lights and shadows. And as we look upon the world around us, and upon the thousand forms of human misery, there is a gladness in our deep thanksgiving.

A year goes by; but it leaves no added shadow on our hearth-stone. The vines clamber and flourish; the oaks are winning age and grandeur. Little Carry is blooming into the pretty coyness of girlhood; and Jamie, with his dark hair and flashing eyes, is the pride of his mother.

There is no alloy to pleasure but the remembrance of poor little Paul. And even that, chastened as it is with years, is rather a grateful memorial that our life is not all here, than a grief that weighs upon our hearts.

Sometimes, leaving little Carry and Jamie to their play, we wander at twilight to the willow-tree beneath which our drowned boy sleeps calmly for the Great Awaking. It is a Sunday in the week-day of our life to linger by the little grave, — to hang flowers upon the headstone, and to breathe a prayer that our little Paul may sleep well in the arms of Him who loveth children!

And her heart, and my heart, knit together by sorrow as they had been knit by joy,—a silver thread mingled with the gold, — follow the dead one to the Land that is before us, until at last we come to reckon the boy as living in the new home which, when this is old, shall be ours also. And my spirit, speaking to his spirit in the evening watches, seems to say joyfully,— so joyfully that the tears half choke the utterance, — " Paul, my boy, we will be *there!* "

And the mother, turning her face to mine, so that I see the moisture in her eye, and catch its heavenly look, whispers softly,— so softly that an angel might have said it, — " Yes, dear, we will be THERE!"

The night had now come, and my day under the oaks was ended. But a crimson belt yet lingered over the horizon, though the stars were out.

A line of shaggy mist lay along the surface of the brook. I took my gun from beside the tree, and my shot-pouch from its limb, and whistling for Carlo, — as if it had been Tray, — I strolled over the bridge, and down the lane, to the old house under the elms.

I dreamed pleasant dreams that night;—for I dreamed that my Reverie was real.